# Urban Bosses, Machines, and Progressive Reformers

# PROBLEMS IN AMERICAN CIVILIZATION

*Under the editorial direction of*
Edwin C. Rozwenc

# Urban Bosses, Machines, and Progressive Reformers

*Edited and with an Introduction by*

**Bruce M. Stave**
University of Connecticut

**D. C. HEATH AND COMPANY**
Lexington, Massachusetts Toronto London

For
Channing,
Boss of the Teddy Bear Ring
and
Sandye, His Mama and
Chief Political Adviser

# CONTENTS

## I TURN OF THE CENTURY OBSERVATIONS

## II THE MACHINE AND ITS FUNCTIONS

# III BOSSES AND REFORMERS

# IV BUSINESSMEN, SOCIALISTS, AND MUNICIPAL REFORM

# INTRODUCTION

"Boss" and "machine" have often connoted, at their best, devious political maneuvering, graft and corruption, and, at their worst, evil incarnate. To this day, if an American candidate is labeled the puppet of the "bosses" or a product of the "machine," he must work doubly hard to convince the public of his purity. During the Progressive era, which spanned approximately the first two decades of the twentieth century, crusades against bossism stood high on the list of urban reform. The purification of politics meant removing power from the clutches of the machines and vesting it in the hands of the pristine reformers. On closer look, however, the dichotomy between boss and reformer may not be as absolute as some Progressives perceived.

The same may be said for the relationship between the political machines and business. Reform has often been seen as an uprising against business, which used its growing wealth to buy from the corrupt machines franchises, charters, and privileges. These, in turn, permitted businessmen to amass even greater fortunes in an increasingly industrialized and urbanized America. Hence, Progressive theory holds that corrupted politics and corrupting business marched hand in hand.

Following the bosses and the businessmen in this alleged parade against good government were the masses of immigrants who had come to America during the final decades of the nineteenth century and the earliest years of the twentieth. Between 1882 and 1914, approximately 20 million immigrants came to the United States; 1,285,000 arrived during the crest year, 1907, alone. They searched for security in an uncertain new world, and the local politicians answered their needs. A food basket at Christmas, a job, aid to one's son in trouble with the truant officer, and many other services wedded the immigrant to the local machine. The boss only required as *quid pro quo* the vote of an individual—or the collective vote of a grateful family. Bosses like Tammany Hall's Richard Croker and Chicago's ward politicians Hinky Dink Kenna and Bathhouse John Coughlin depended upon such support. On the other hand, the immigrant and the Progressive reformers were estranged from each other. The immigrant was suspicious of the often upper-class reformer; conversely, as Croker noted, "There is not a mugwump in the city who would shake hands with [the immigrants]." Socialist reformers, who frequently defended the immigrants, were all too often limited in their municipal programs.

The Progressive interpretation of urban politics raises several questions. Were the boss and his political machine really evil and immoral? What were their functions and why did they arise in the first place? Were the methods and the goals of the bosses diametrically opposed to those of the reformers? Did the immigrants ever support reform legislation? What was the role of business in instituting urban reform during the Progressive era? Did Socialist municipal reformers differ in their program from Progressives? What were some of the more important urban reforms to which all of these groups addressed themselves?

This volume, divided into four sections, attempts to answer these questions. The first section presents views by contemporaries of the period of urban political machines and bosses. One picture, especially if it is a devastatingly satirical political cartoon, is often worth a thousand words. Thomas Nast's poison-pen portraits of Boss Tweed in *Harper's Weekly,* first appearing in 1868, helped set the stage for the dismal view that contemporaries took of bosses during the last part of the nineteenth and early years of the twentieth century. As Alexander B. Callow, Jr., a recent student of the Tweed Ring, has observed, Tweed recognized the potency of these attacks and remarked, "I don't care a straw for your newspaper articles, my constituents don't know how to read, but they can't help seeing them damned pictures."

This image of the corrupt boss took hold. When James Bryce, author of the first selection in this volume, left his native England to visit the United States during the late nineteenth century, he found local government here a conspicuous failure. Lord Bryce's *American Commonwealth,* first published in 1888 and written primarily for Europeans, takes a jaundiced view of the boss and the machine. His attack raises the issue of why bossism came into existence. Was American municipal politics based on tangibles (the spoils system) rather than ideology and did this situation give rise to the boss system? Or were a largely immigrant electorate and an apathetic native stock of "good citizens" the real reasons for the existence of machine politics?

Another contemporary observer, Jane Addams, the Progressive founder of Hull House, did believe that there was a strong connection between the immigrant neighborhood and the local boss. For his constituency, the boss was "a good friend and neighbor" and therefore more appealing to the people than the settlement-house worker, frequently an outsider who took a condescending view toward the people with whom he or she worked. In many respects the same problems of identification that faced the young community organizers of the 1960's and early 1970's were confronted more than a half century earlier by the Progressive settlement workers. In effect, it was the local ward boss who answered the earlier need for community control over decision-making.

Jane Addams fought the local machines, but understood the reasons for their neighborhood support; muckraking journalist Lincoln Steffens exposed their corrupt side and laid much of the blame at the feet of business. For Steffens, it was more an expanding and greedy American business, paying for special favors from the bosses, that caused corruption, than the immigrant mass base that kept the machines well oiled and functioning. His *The Shame of the Cities* stands as a classic Progressive statement, or perhaps overstatement, regarding the problems of urban America during that era.

George Washington Plunkitt, himself a Tammany chieftain, obviously disagreed with Steffens; he saw a good deal of value in machine politics and political bosses. According to Plunkitt, bosses helped to preserve the nation. While reform administrations were ripped by factionalism, the boss brought unity to government. When Lincoln Steffens asked Tammany Boss Richard Croker, "Why must there be a boss when we've got a mayor and a council?" Croker replied:

> That's why. . . . It's because there's a mayor and a council and judges and—a hundred other men to deal with. A government is nothing but a business with a lot of officials who check and cross-check one another and who come and go, there this year, out the next. A businessman wants to do business with one man and one who is always there to remember to carry out the business.

Moreover, as far as ethics were concerned, Plunkitt believed the boss would be a fool not to take advantage of "honest graft" as opposed to "dishonest graft." An example of the latter might be extorting large sums to "protect" the operations of gamblers and prostitutes. "Honest graft," on the other hand, might be buying up seemingly useless land that you had learned through privileged information was scheduled for eminent domain. As Plunkitt said, "I seen my opportunities and I took 'em." Yet he and other local politicians believed they were justified in taking such opportunities, because this was often the only payment they received for their services to the neighborhood and the city.

Just how accurate are the observations of the contemporary observers? Can individuals who live through a period of history see the trees from the forest? Plunkitt framed machine politics in a favorable perspective, but the other three observers, wearing the spectacles of Progressive dogma, found much to condemn about that institution of urban life. In the second section, a sociologist and four historians attempt to analyze the boss and the machine without drawing moral judgments.

Robert Merton, the sociologist, claims that moralism often clouds one's perspective. He investigates how the machine persists as an American institution, even though its ethics often run counter to prevailing moral attitudes. In pursuing the answer to this question, Merton develops a functional analysis of boss politics. If the machine served certain latent functions, as described by Merton, the student might consider what role, beside an illicit one, crime serves. If the observer divorces himself from the moral issues, does he thereby distort his understanding as much as if he saw everything in terms of good and evil?

Eric McKitrick, in "The Study of Corruption," extends Merton's model and explores the pattern's application to mid-twentieth century America. For McKitrick, the machine is a dynamic, changing organism which has evolved during the twentieth century. Assuming one of its several latent functions is to respond to the welfare needs of immigrants and to serve as a ladder of social mobility for ethnic groups blocked from other means of rising within society, what does this mean for contemporary urban politics? McKitrick asks whether new ethnic groups will replace older ones in controlling and engaging in machine politics. One should consider the increasing number of black mayors elected during the 1960's and early 1970's before answering this question in the negative.

Should the boss be a model to consider for those politicians who have been elected to municipal office in recent years? Monte Calvert contends that the boss should serve as such a model. Calvert is more interested in the manifest functions of the machine, such as the economical and efficient administration of a big city, than in its latent functions; he sees the boss as an example of the unspecialized professional, who is best able to cope with the problems of today's cities.

The problems of yesterday's cities were handled by men like Boss Tweed, whom Seymour Mandelbaum views as uniting a highly fragmented nineteenth-century New York in the only manner in which it could be united—through the big payoff. In a society that was based upon the free operations of the marketplace, Tweed answered the simple but central questions: "How much will you supply?" and "How much will you pay?" These were also the questions that the Chicago politicians studied by Joel Tarr concerned themselves with. Tarr demonstrates how the local politicians used their political influence for economic gain and why their social backgrounds made them see politics as a vehicle for advancement rather than as a means of social reform. For him, the urban politician was an entrepreneur who believed in George Washington Plunkitt's assertion that "when a man works in politics he should get something out of it." At this point, the student might contemplate whether the social costs to the public, such as the payment of graft, were worth the benefits brought to urban America by the bosses and their machines.

Were all the bosses like the ones that Tarr describes—interested in little but economic gain? Or did they sometimes support reform legislation? How pristine were the reformers who opposed them? The third section, "Bosses and Reformers," investigates the inter-action of these two groups, and examines the problem of how cities develop.

How do cities grow from the center outerwards, from the walking city to the larger metropolis? First, there must be the desire of individuals to leave the central city; this raises the question of why they wish to do so. Then, there must be a means of spreading into outlying areas. The urban transportation revolution of the late nineteenth century provided this means. Using Boston as a case study, Samuel Bass Warner, Jr., has shown that while the outer boundary of dense settlement in that city in 1873 stood two and one-half miles from its City Hall by the 1890's, with the advent of the electric street railway, the outer border of settlement ranged to at least six miles. The same process of growth occurred in other American cities during the late nineteenth century.

Many fled the central city to get away from the new industry and the environmental problems it created, from other kinds of people, from overcrowding, and from crime—a situation that might seem familiar to today's reader. During the late nineteenth century the new suburban neighborhoods, which in our own time have become part of most central cities, epitomized Arcadia. According to Richard C. Wade, author of the first selection in the segment on "Bosses and Reformers," it was in the newer parts of the city that reform took strongest hold. The older city dwellers, often white Anglo-Saxon Protestants who could afford to move to the newer areas, saw the central city as the bastion of the boss and his immi-grant following. Hence, the reform movement was a struggle of the periphery against the center to determine which group would shape the life of the city.

When evaluating the periphery-versus-center thesis, students might do well to consider whether this ecological approach, in which residence alone is the basis of the city's social and political experience, is more or less appropriate than a model which makes residence a function of social and economic variables such as ethnicity, race, religion, and occupation. What is the significance of many of these suburban residents still working in the center of the city even after they have moved their homes away from that area?

Zane Miller, who studies a Cincinnati divided into Circle, Zone, and Hilltops, follows the periphery-versus-center model. However, Miller modifies Wade's sharp dichotomy between boss and reformer by suggesting that Boss Cox's original support rested with the periphery against the center. That is, the boss's early coalition included many of the outlying neighborhoods. Perhaps this was because Cox brought order to a city in disorder, while instituting a broad reform program that ranged from professionalizing the police force to supporting the growth of the University of Cincinnati, to initiating housing regulations, to lowering the municipal tax rate, to strengthening the office of mayor and streamlining city government.

Could this be the same corrupt and evil boss that some of the contemporary observers discussed? Obviously, Boss Cox acted the role of reformer, at least in certain times during his career. Thus, it might not be surprising to learn that Tammany Hall, under the leadership of Charles Francis Murphy, supported Progressive reform in New York State before and after World War I. Why was this so? J. Joseph Huthmacher informs us that "Murphy's progressivism was in large part the manifestation of a practical politician's self-defense tactics." He supported reform because his constituency wanted him to. This fact raises the question of whether in politics it is the people who follow the leader or the leader who follows the people. Huthmacher also suggests another important issue about Progressivism. What role did the urban, immigrant, lower-class population play during that era? If it did not oppose reform, although the unmodified periphery-versus-center thesis suggests that it did, then were the working class ethnics part of a Progressive coalition? Did they initiate reform or simply support the reform efforts of others? When considering a movement such as Progressivism, is it important to differentiate between the initiators and the supporters of reform to explain its impact on American society?

If bosses and their immigrant following were not loath to support reform measures, did reformers ever employ the tactics most usually associated with machine politics? Melvin G. Holli tells us that the reform mayor of Detroit during the 1890's, Hazen S. Pingree, learned to use machine methods and created his own well-disciplined political machine to further his objectives of social reform. The fact that the mechanics of organization were as important to the reformer as they were to the boss leads us to ponder the definition of a political machine. Is it simply an efficiently run organization, or is there something else that differentiates it from an operation such as Pingree's? Must goals as well as methods, type of personnel, and hierarchical structure be considered before we argue that there may be little difference between reformers and bosses?

According to Allen F. Davis, in some city wards, like Chicago's seventeenth, where there was no single powerful boss, Progressive settlement-house reformers successfully built their own political organization. On the other hand, Jane Addams and her followers had less luck in that city's nineteenth ward, where Boss Johnny Powers was firmly entrenched. In Boston's ninth ward, the social workers cooperated with the local boss, who needed allies against other city politicians, and thus won him over to reform. Local conditions colored the outcome of each one of these battles between reformers and bosses. Nevertheless, the reformers became very much engaged in politics, and, as we have seen, some of the machine politicians engaged in reform.

During the Progressive era there were several types of reform, generally categorized as either economic, social welfare, or structural. The first two readings in the final section, "Businessmen, Socialists, and Municipal Reform," concern structural reforms such as the city manager and city commission forms of government, the establishment of city-wide school boards, and the city-wide election of councilmen as opposed to elections by neighborhoods. Both the selection by Samuel P. Hays and the one by James Weinstein indicate that business gave a great deal of support to much of this government change—in fact, it generally initiated it. Why was this the case? Why would the values of efficiency and rationalization associated with such reforms make them appealing to businessmen? If they were the chief advocates of programs like the city manager form of government, what about Lincoln Steffens' assertion that business was largely responsible for political corruption? In sum, was urban Progressivism an uprising against business and the machine, or was it actually inspired by business?

Moreover, Progressives often claimed that a goal of their reform was the broadening of democracy. Yet Hays, in an attempt to separate rhetoric from reality, finds that the new industrial business elite's attempt to take power from the neighborhoods (often represented by the boss and the machine) and place it on the city-wide level did anything but that. Paradoxically, the ideology of Progressivism was the extension of political control, but its practice often resulted in the concentration of political control. An understanding of the centralizing of decision-making in big cities during the Progressive era will help one to perceive the struggle over decentralization in contemporary urban America. Is the battle for community control of school boards in a city like New York a reaction to the centralization that occurred in many cities more than a half century ago? When urban blacks call for community control, are they really saying they want the same representation that ethnic groups once had through the machines and the neighborhood election of city councilmen?

One group that opposed the business-inspired manager and commission plans during the Progressive era was the municipal Socialists, who had elected 74 mayors or other city officials in 1911. It found that the elimination of ward representation meant the elimination of minority representation in city government and the concomitant weakening of minority power. Yet, in other aspects of their programs the business reformers and the Socialists came to share similar views. The business effort to rationalize urban government and increase public services without increasing the tax rate often led, as Weinstein explains, to municipal ownership, increased planning, and even social reform. The groups may have differed over who was to administer such programs and what their ultimate purpose was, but the programs turned out to be similar.

What does this tell us about municipal Socialism in America? The selections by both Louis Heaton Pink and David A. Shannon help to provide answers to that question and insight into the reformist nature of Socialism in our cities. The Socialists only gained power in cities where they were able to build their own political machines. Once the Socialists were in power, the constraints of office channeled most of their efforts into what became known as "sewer socialism"—a very limited brand of Socialism, indeed.

Finally, we should consider whether urban politics and reform have changed very much since the Progressive era. The last selection, by Roy Lubove, indicates that Pittsburgh's post-World War II urban "Renaissance" was business inspired much as the Progressive reforms discussed by Hays. If this demonstrates some continuity, at least in the type of business-elite reformer who was active in both periods, what of the continuity of machine politics? Have the bosses and the machine long since suffered the "last hurrah," or do they still exist, perhaps in some changed form, today? When a politician calls his opponent a "boss," when a newspaper editorializes against the local "machine," do the words have the same meaning today as they did at the turn of the century?

As the student seeks to understand machine and reform politics in America's cities he will find the issues complex and the historical differences between bosses and reformers ambiguous. Nevertheless, one fact should be obvious: the manichean belief that one group was corrupt and the other pure, that one bilked the public and the other benefited the people, is historically inaccurate.

# Conflict of Opinion

## Turn of the Century Observations:

An army led by a council seldom conquers: it must have a commander-in-chief, who settles disputes, decides in emergencies, inspires fear or attachment. The head of the Ring is such a commander. He dispenses places, rewards the loyal, punishes the mutinous, concocts schemes, negotiates treaties. He generally avoids publicity, preferring the substance to the pomp of power, and is all the more dangerous because he sits, like a spider, hidden in the midst of his web. He is a Boss.

LORD JAMES BRYCE

". . . Have you ever thought what would become of the country if the bosses were put out of business, and their places were taken by a lot of cart-tail orators and college graduates? It would mean chaos. It would be just like takin' a lot of dry-goods clerks and settin' them to run express trains on the New York Central Railroad. It makes my heart bleed to think of it."

GEORGE WASHINGTON PLUNKITT

## The Machine and Its Functions:

Proceeding from the functional view, therefore, that we should *ordinarily* (not invariably) expect persistent social patterns and social structures to perform positive functions *which are at the time not adequately fulfilled by other existing patterns and structures,* the thought occurs that perhaps this publicly maligned organization is, *under present conditions,* satisfying basic latent functions.

ROBERT K. MERTON

All one can say about Tweed is that he was predictable. He united the elements in a divided society in the only manner in which they could be united: by paying them off. Attracted to a scorned profession, he acted with scorn for conventional social ethics. Like so many American entrepreneurs, he maximized his short-run profits and then got out.

SEYMOUR MANDELBAUM

## Bosses and Reformers:

Reform found its major spokesman and greatest support in middle-class residential areas on the outer ring of the city. . . . The boss's strength was in the city's core where the newcomers had settled. . . . Hence, reform was a movement of the periphery against the center.

RICHARD C. WADE

What, then, was Boss Cox's role in politics and government in the new city? He helped create and manage a voluntary political-action organization which bridged the racial and cultural chasms between the Circle, Zone, and Hilltops. He and his allies were able to bring positive and moderate reform government to Cincinnati and to mitigate the conflict and disorder which accompanied the emergence of the new city. . . . Cox, it seems, said more than he realized when, in 1892, he remarked that a boss was "not necessarily a public enemy."

ZANE L. MILLER

Although Pingree was loath to admit it, his effectiveness as an urban reformer was undoubtedly due in part to his creation of a well-disciplined political machine.

MELVIN G. HOLLI

. . . But whether [the settlement-house workers] were participants in local politics or merely observers, and regardless of whether they defeated the ward boss or were defeated by him, [they] invariably came to appreciate the usefulness of the politician and to learn from him, even as they despaired his lack of honesty and civic pride. They were among the first to analyze the source of the bosses' strength.

ALLEN F. DAVIS

## Businessmen, Socialists, and Municipal Reform:

The movement for reform in municipal government, therefore, constituted an attempt by upper-class, advanced professional, and large business groups to take formal political power from the previously dominant lower and middle-class elements so that they might advance their own conceptions of desirable public policy. These two groups came from entirely different urban worlds, and the political system fashioned by one was no longer acceptable to the other.

SAMUEL P. HAYS

The Milwaukee Socialists had a party organization in every precinct to get their supporters registered, get them to the polls, and get their ballots counted. The party machinery could get literature into every house in Milwaukee within a few hours and in the proper language, English, German or Polish. Victor Berger was the "boss" behind all these party activities and one of the bossiest "bosses" in a nation that had developed the art to a high degree.

DAVID A. SHANNON

# I TURN OF THE CENTURY OBSERVATIONS

## James Bryce
# SETTING THE STEREOTYPE

*After his visit to America in the late nineteenth century, the Englishman Lord James Bryce described local government in the United States as a conspicuous failure. His discussion of "Rings and Bosses" in* The American Commonwealth *helped to establish the image of the political boss as interested only in the material rewards of politics, taking advantage of the apathy of the "good citizens" of the community to manipulate an ignorant mass electorate. For Bryce, the boss had little social value.*

In a Ring there is usually some one person who holds more strings in his hand than do the others. Like them he has worked himself up to power from small beginnings, gradually extending the range of his influence over the mass of workers, and knitting close bonds with influential men outside as well as inside politics, perhaps with great financiers or railway magnates, whom he can oblige, and who can furnish him with funds. At length his superior skill, courage, and force of will make him, as such gifts always do make their possessor, dominant among his fellows. An army led by a council seldom conquers: it must have a commander-in-chief, who settles disputes, decides in emergencies, inspires fear or attachment. The head of the Ring is such a commander. He dispenses places, rewards the loyal, punishes the mutinous, concocts schemes, negotiates treaties. He generally avoids publicity, preferring the substance to the pomp of power, and is all the more dangerous because he sits, like a spider, hidden in the midst of his web. He is a Boss.

Although the career I have sketched is that whereby most Bosses have risen to greatness, some attain it by a shorter path. There have been brilliant instances of persons stepping at once on to the higher rungs of the ladder in virtue of their audacity and energy, especially if coupled with oratorical power. The first theatre of such a man's successes may have been the stump rather than the primary: he will then become potent in conventions, and either by hectoring or by plausible address, for both have their value, spring into popular favour, and make himself necessary to the party

From James Bryce, *The American Commonwealth*, Vol. II (New York, 1893), pp. 109–116, 120–121.

**3**

managers. It is of course a gain to a Ring to have among them a man of popular gifts, because he helps to conceal the odious features of their rule, gilding it by his rhetoric, and winning the applause of the masses who stand outside the circle of workers. However, the position of the rhetorical boss is less firmly rooted than that of the intriguing boss, and there have been instances of his suddenly falling to rise no more.

A great city is the best soil for the growth of a Boss, because it contains the largest masses of manageable voters as well as numerous offices and plentiful opportunities for jobbing. But a whole State sometimes falls under the dominion of one intriguer. To govern so large a territory needs high abilities; and the State boss is always an able man, somewhat more of a politician, in the European sense, than a city boss need be. He dictates State nominations, and through his lieutenants controls State and sometimes Congressional conventions, being in diplomatic relations with the chief city bosses and local rings in different parts of the State. His power over them mainly springs from his influence with the Federal executive and in Congress. He is usually, almost necessarily, a member of Congress, probably a senator, and can procure, or at any rate can hinder, such legislation as the local leaders desire or dislike. The President cannot ignore him, and the President's ministers, however little they may like him, find it worth while to gratify him with Federal appointments for persons he recommends, because the local votes he controls may make all the difference to their own prospects of getting some day a nomination for the presidency. Thus he uses his Congressional position to secure State influence, and his State influence to strengthen his Federal position. Sometimes however he is rebuffed by the powers at Washington and then his State thanes fly from him. Sometimes he quarrels with a powerful city boss, and then honest men come by their own.

[It must not be supposed that the members of Rings, or the great Boss himself, are wicked men. They are the offspring of a system. Their morality is that of their surroundings. They see a door open to wealth and power, and they walk in. The obligations of patriotism or duty to the public are not disregarded by them, for these obligations have never been present to their minds.] A State boss is usually a native American and a person of some education, who avoids the grosser forms of corruption, though he has to wink at them when practised by his friends. He may be a man of personal integrity.[1] A city boss is often of foreign birth and humble origin; he has grown up in an atmosphere of oaths and cocktails: ideas of honour and purity are as strange to him as ideas about the nature of the currency and the incidence of taxation: politics is merely a means for getting and distributing places. "What," said an ingenuous delegate at one of the National Conventions at Chicago in 1880, "what are we here for except the offices?" It is no wonder if he helps himself from the city treasury and allows his minions to do so. Sometimes he does not rob, and, like Clive, wonders at his own moderation. And even the city Boss improves as he rises in the world. Like a tree growing out of a dust heap, the higher he gets, the cleaner do his boughs and leaves become. America is a country where vulgarity is sealed off more easily than in England, and where the general air of good nature softens the asperities of power. Some city bosses are men from whose decorous exterior and unobtrusive manners no one would divine either their sordid beginnings or their noxious trade. As for the State boss, whose talents are probably greater to begin with, he must be of very coarse metal if he does not take a certain polish from the society of Washington.

A city Ring works somewhat as follows. When the annual or biennial city or State elections come round, its members meet to discuss the apportionment of offices. Each may desire something for himself, unless indeed he is already fully provided for, and anyhow desires something for his friends. The common sort are provided for with small places in the gift of some official, down to the place of a policeman or doorkeeper or messenger, which is thought good enough for a common "ward worker." Better men receive clerkships or the promise of a place in the custom-house or post-office to be obtained from the Federal authorities. Men still more important aspire to the elective posts, seats in the State legislature, a city aldermanship or commissionership, perhaps even a seat in Congress. All the posts that will have to be filled at the coming elections are considered with the object of bringing out a party ticket, *i.e.* a list of candidates to be supported by the party at the

---

[1] So too a rural boss is often quite pure, and blameworthy rather for his intriguing methods than for his aims.

polls when its various nominations have been successfully run
through the proper conventions. Some leading man, or probably
the Boss himself, sketches out an allotment of places; and when
this allotment has been worked out fully, it results in a Slate, *i.e.*
a complete draft list of candidates to be proposed for the various
offices.[2] It may happen that the slate does not meet everybody's
wishes. Some member of the ring or some local boss—most members of a ring are bosses each in his own district, as the members
of a cabinet are heads of the departments of state, or as the cardi-
nals are bishops of dioceses near Rome and priests and deacons
of her parish churches—may complain that he and his friends
have not been adequately provided for, and may demand more. In
that case the slate will probably be modified a little to ensure good
feeling and content; and will then be presented to the Convention.

. . . Discipline is very strict in this army. Even city politicians must
have a moral code and moral standard. It is not the code of an
ordinary unprofessional citizen. It does not forbid falsehood, or
malversation, or ballot stuffing, or "repeating." But it denounces
apathy or cowardice, disobedience, and above all, treason to the
party. Its typical virtue is "solidity," unity of heart, mind, and effort
among the workers, unquestioning loyalty to the party leaders,
and devotion to the party ticket. He who takes his own course is a
Kicker or Bolter; and is punished not only sternly but vindictively.
The path of promotion is closed to him; he is turned out of the
primary, and forbidden to hope for a delegacy to a convention; he
is dismissed from any office he holds which the Ring can command.
Dark stories are even told of a secret police which will pursue the
culprit who has betrayed his party, and of mysterious disappear-
ances of men whose testimony against the Ring was feared.
Whether there is any foundation for such tales I do not undertake
to say. But true it is that the bond between the party chiefs and
their followers is very close and very seldom broken. What the

[2] A pleasant story is told of a former Boss of New York State, who sat with his
vassals just before the convention, preparing the Slate. There were half a dozen or
more State offices for which nominations were to be made. The names were with
deliberation selected and set down, with the exception of the very unimportant
place of State Prison Inspector. One of his subordinates ventured to call the
attention of the Boss to what he supposed to be an inadvertence, and asked who
was to be the man for that place, to which the great man answered, with an
indulgent smile, "I guess we will leave *that* to the convention."

client was to his patron at Rome, what the vassal was to his lord in the Middle Ages, that the heelers and workers are to their boss in these great transatlantic cities. They render a personal feudal service, which their suzerain repays with the gift of a livelihood; and the relation is all the more cordial because the lord bestows what costs him nothing, while the vassal feels that he can keep his post only by the favour of the lord.

European readers must again be cautioned against drawing for themselves too dark a picture of the Boss. He is not a demon. He is not regarded with horror even by those "good citizens" who strive to shake off his yoke. He is not necessarily either corrupt or mendacious, though he grasps at place, power, and wealth. He is a leader to whom certain peculiar social and political conditions have given a character dissimilar from the party leaders whom Europe knows. It is worth while to point out in what the dissimilarity consists.

A Boss needs fewer showy gifts than a European demogogue. His special theatre is neither the halls of the legislature nor the platform, but the committee-room. A power of rough and ready repartee, or a turn for florid declamation, will help him; but he can dispense with both. What he needs are the arts of intrigue and that knowledge of men which teaches him when to bully, when to cajole, whom to attract by the hope of gain, whom by appeals to party loyalty. Nor are so-called "social gifts" unimportant. The lower sort of city politicians congregate in clubs and bar-rooms; and as much of the cohesive strength of the smaller party organizations arises from their being also social bodies, so also much of the power which liquor dealers exercise is due to the fact that "heelers" and "workers" spend their evenings in drinking places, and that meetings for political purposes are held there. Of the 1007 primaries and conventions of all parties held in New York City preparatory to the elections of 1884, 633 took place in liquor saloons. A Boss ought therefore to be hail fellow well met with those who frequent these places, not fastidious in his tastes, fond of a drink and willing to stand one, jovial in manners, and ready to oblige even a humble friend.

The aim of a Boss is not so much fame as power, and power not so much over the conduct of affairs as over persons. Patronage is what he chiefly seeks, patronage understood in the largest sense in which it covers the disposal of lucrative contracts and other modes of enrichment as well as salaried places. The dependants who surround him desire wealth, or at least a livelihood; his business is to find this for them, and in doing so he strengthens his own position.[3] It is as the bestower of riches that he holds his position, like the leader of a band of condottieri in the fifteenth century.

The interest of a Boss in political questions is usually quite secondary. Here and there one may be found who is a politician in the European sense, who, whether sincerely or not, professes to be interested in some measure affecting the welfare of the country. But the attachment of the ringster is usually given wholly to the concrete party, that is to the men who compose it, regarded as office-holders or office-seekers; and there is often not even a profession of zeal for any party doctrine. As a noted politician once happily observed, "There are no politics in politics." Among bosses, therefore, there is little warmth of party spirit. The typical boss regards the boss of the other party much as counsel for the plaintiff regards counsel for the defendant. They are professionally opposed, but not necessarily personally hostile. Between bosses there need be no more enmity than results from the fact that the one has got what the other wishes to have. Accordingly it sometimes happens that there is a good understanding between the chiefs of opposite parties in cities; they will even go the length of making a joint "deal," *i.e.* of arranging for a distribution of offices whereby some of the friends of one shall get places, the residue being left for the friends of the other. A well-organized city party has usually a disposable vote which can be so cast under the

---

[3] "A Boss is able to procure positions for many of his henchmen on horse-railroads, the elevated roads, quarry works, etc. Great corporations are peculiarly subject to the attacks of demagogues, and they find it greatly to their interest to be on good terms with the leader in each district who controls the vote of the assemblyman and alderman; and therefore the former is pretty sure that a letter of recommendation from him on behalf of any applicant for work will receive most favorable consideration. The leader also is continually helping his supporters out of difficulties, pecuniary and otherwise: he lends them a dollar now and then, helps out, when possible, such of their kinsmen as get into the clutches of the law, gets a hold over such of them as have done wrong and are afraid of being exposed, and learns to mix bullying judiciously with the rendering of service."—Mr. Theodore Roosevelt, in the *Century* magazine for Nov. 1886.

directions of the managers as to effect this, or any other desired result. The appearance of hostility must, of course, be maintained for the benefit of the public; but as it is for the interest of both parties to make and keep these private bargains, they are usually kept when made, though it is seldom possible to prove the fact.

[The real hostility of the Boss is not to the opposite party, but to other factions within his own party.]

\*     \*     \*

It has been pointed out that rings and bosses are the product not of democracy, but of a particular form of democratic government, acting under certain peculiar conditions. They belong to democratic government, as the old logicians would say, not *simpliciter* but *secundum quid*: they are not of its essence, but are merely separable accidents. We have seen that these conditions are—

[The existence of a Spoils System (= paid offices given and taken away for party reasons).

Opportunities for illicit gains arising out of the possession of office.

The presence of a mass of ignorant and pliable voters.

The insufficient participation in politics of the "good citizens."]

If these be the true causes or conditions producing the phenomenon, we may expect to find it most fully developed in the places where the conditions exist in fullest measure, less so where they are more limited, absent where they do not exist.

A short examination of the facts will show that such is the case.

It may be thought that the Spoils System is a constant, existing everywhere, and therefore not admitting of the application of this method of concomitant variations. That system does no doubt prevail over every State of the Union, but it is not everywhere an equally potent factor, for in some cities the offices are much better paid than in others, and the revenues which their occupants control are larger. In some small communities the offices, or most of them, are not paid at all. Hence this factor varies scarcely less than the others.

We may therefore say with truth that all of the four conditions

above named are most fully present in great cities. Some of the
offices are highly paid; many give facilities for lucrative jobbing;
and the unpaid officers are sometimes the most apt to abuse these
facilities. The voters are so numerous that a strong and active organization is needed to drill them; the majority so ignorant as to
be easily led. [The best citizens are engrossed in business and cannot give to political work the continuous attention it demands.] Such
are the phenomena of New York, Philadelphia, Chicago, Brooklyn,
St. Louis, Cincinnati, San Francisco, Baltimore, and New Orleans.
In these cities Ring-and-bossdom has attained its amplest growth,
overshadowing the whole field of politics.

*Jane Addams*

# WHY THE WARD BOSS RULES

*The reformers and settlement-house workers of Jane Addams' Hull House
soon came into conflict with the alderman boss of Chicago's nineteenth
ward. In April 1898 The Outlook magazine reprinted a portion of an article
by Miss Addams which had, in part, precipitated the clash. The magazine
"selected those passages which show why the Alderman, who is the most
obedient servant of the monopolies, holds a thus far impregnable position
in a ward composed of the very poor." In this selection, Jane Addams
recognizes that the ward boss performed a social-welfare service for his
immigrant following, a service which the reformers frequently could not
deliver because of bureaucratic red tape or a lack of identification with the
community.*

Primitive people, such as the South Italian peasants who live in the
Nineteenth Ward, deep down in their hearts admire nothing so much
as the good man. The successful candidate must be a good man according to the standards of his constituents. He must not attempt
to hold up a morality beyond them, nor must he attempt to reform
or change the standard. If he believes what they believe, and does
what they are all cherishing a secret ambition to do, he will dazzle

From Jane Addams, "Why the Ward Boss Rules," *The Outlook,* 58 (April 2, 1898),
pp. 879–882.

them by his success and win their confidence. Any one who has lived among poorer people cannot fail to be impressed with their constant kindness to each other; that unfailing response to the needs and distresses of their neighbors, even when in danger of bankruptcy themselves. This is their reward for living in the midst of poverty. They have constant opportunities for self-sacrifice and generosity, to which, as a rule, they respond. A man stands by his friend when he gets too drunk to take care of himself, when he loses his wife or child, when he is evicted for non-payment of rent, when he is arrested for a petty crime. It seems to such a man entirely fitting that his Alderman should do the same thing on a larger scale—that he should help a constituent out of trouble just because he is in trouble, irrespective of the justice involved.

The Alderman, therefore, bails out his constituents when they are arrested, or says a good word to the police justice when they appear before him for trial; uses his "pull" with the magistrate when they are likely to be fined for a civil misdemeanor, or sees what he can do to "fix up matters" with the State's attorney when the charge is really a serious one.

Because of simple friendliness, the Alderman is expected to pay rent for the hard-pressed tenant when no rent is forthcoming, to find jobs when work is hard to get, to procure and divide among his constituents all the places which he can seize from the City Hall. The Alderman of the Nineteenth Ward at one time made the proud boast that he had two thousand six hundred people in his ward upon the public pay-roll. This, of course, included day-laborers, but each one felt under distinct obligations to him for getting the job.

If we recollect, further, that the franchise-seeking companies pay respectful heed to the applicants backed by the Alderman, the question of voting for the successful man becomes as much an industrial as a political one. An Italian laborer wants a job more than anything else, and quite simply votes for the man who promises him one.

The Alderman may himself be quite sincere in his acts of kindness. In certain stages of moral evolution, a man is incapable of unselfish action the results of which will not benefit some one of his acquaintances; still more, of conduct that does not aim to assist any individual whatsoever; and it is a long step in moral progress to appreciate the work done by the individual for the community.

The Alderman gives presents at weddings and christenings. He seizes these days of family festivities for making friends. It is easiest to reach people in the holiday mood of expansive good will, but on their side it seems natural and kindly that he should do it. The Alderman procures passes from the railroads when his constituents wish to visit friends or to attend the funerals of distant relatives; he buys tickets galore for benefit entertainments given for a widow or a consumptive in peculiar distress; he contributes to prizes which are awarded to the handsomest lady or the most popular man. At a church bazaar, for instance, the Alderman finds the stage all set for his dramatic performance. When others are spending pennies he is spending dollars. Where anxious relatives are canvassing to secure votes for the two most beautiful children who are being voted upon, he recklessly buys votes from both sides, and laughingly declines to say which one he likes the best, buying off the young lady who is persistently determined to find out, with five dollars for the flower bazaar, the posies, of course, to be sent to the sick of the parish. The moral atmosphere of a bazaar suits him exactly. He murmurs many times, "Never mind; the money all goes to the poor," or, "It is all straight enough if the church gets it."

There is something archaic in a community of simple people in their attitude towards death and burial. Nothing so easy to collect money for as a funeral. If the Alderman seizes upon festivities for expressions of his good will, much more does he seize upon periods of sorrow. At a funeral he has the double advantage of ministering to a genuine craving for comfort and solace, and at the same time of assisting at an important social function.

In addition to this, there is among the poor, who have few social occasions, a great desire for a well-arranged funeral, the grade of which almost determines their social standing in the neighborhood. The Alderman saves the very poorest of his constituents from that awful horror of burial by the county; he provides carriages for the poor, who otherwise could not have them; for the more prosperous he sends extra carriages, so that they may invite more friends and have a longer procession; for the most prosperous of all there will be probably only a large "flowerpiece." It may be too much to say that all the relatives and friends who ride in the carriages provided by the Alderman's bounty vote for him, but they are certainly influenced by his kindness, and talk of his virtues during the long hours of the ride back and forth from the suburban cemetery. A man who would ask at such a time where all this money comes from would be considered sinister. Many a man at such a time has formulated a lenient judgment of political corruption and has heard kindly speeches which he has remembered on election day. "Ah, well, he has a big Irish heart. He is good to the widow and the fatherless." "He knows the poor better than the big guns who are always about talking civil service and reform."

⌈Indeed, what headway can the notion of civic purity, of honesty of administration, make against this big manifestation of human friendliness, this stalking survival of village kindness? The notions of the civic reformer are negative and impotent before it. The reformers give themselves over largely to criticisms of the present state of affairs, to writing and talking of what the future must be; but their goodness is not dramatic; it is not even concrete and human.⌉

Such an Alderman will keep a standing account with an undertaker, and telephone every week, and sometimes more than once, the kind of outfit he wishes provided for a bereaved constituent, until the sum may roll up into hundreds a year. Such a man understands what the people want, and ministers just as truly to a great human need as the musician or the artist does. I recall an attempt to substitute what we might call a later standard.

A delicate little child was deserted in the Hull House nursery. An investigation showed that it had been born ten days previously in the Cook County Hospital, but no trace could be found of the unfortunate mother. The little thing lived for several weeks, and then, in spite of every care, died. We decided to have it buried by the county, and the wagon was to arrive by eleven o'clock. About nine o'clock in the morning the rumor of this awful deed reached the neighbors. A half-dozen of them came, in a very excited state of mind, to protest. They took up a collection out of their poverty with which to defray a funeral. We were then comparatively new in the neighborhood. We did not realize that we were really shocking a genuine moral sentiment of the community. In our crudeness, we instanced the care and tenderness which had been expended upon the little creature while it was alive; that it had had every attention from a skilled physician and trained nurse; we even intimated that the excited members of the group had not taken part in this, and that it now lay with us to decide that the child should be buried, as it had been born, at the county's expense. It is doubtful whether Hull House has ever done anything which injured it so deeply in the minds of some of its neighbors. We were only forgiven by the most indulgent on the ground that we were spinsters and could not know a mother's heart. No one born and reared in the community could possibly have made a mistake like that. No one who had studied the ethical standards with any care could have bungled so completely.

Last Christmas our Alderman distributed six tons of turkeys, and four or more tons of ducks and geese: but each luckless biped was handed out either by himself or one of his friends with a "Merry Christmas." Inevitably, some families got three or four apiece, but what of that? He had none of the nagging rules of the charitable societies, nor was he ready to declare that, because a man wanted two turkeys for Christmas, he was a scoundrel, who should never be allowed to eat turkey again.

The Alderman's wisdom was again displayed in procuring from down-town friends the sum of three thousand dollars wherewith to uniform and equip a boys' temperance brigade which had been formed in the ward a few months before his campaign. Is it strange that the good leader, whose heart was filled with innocent pride as he looked upon these promising young scions of virtue, should decline to enter into a reform campaign?

The question does, of course, occur to many minds, Where does the money come from with which to dramatize so successfully? The more primitive people accept the truthful statement of its sources without any shock to their moral sense. To their simple minds he gets it "from the rich," and so long as he again gives it out to the poor, as a true Robin Hood, with open hand, they have no objections to offer. Their ethics are quite honestly those of the merry-making foresters. The next less primitive people of the vicinage are quite willing to admit that he leads "the gang" in the

City Council, and sells out the city franchises; that he makes deals with the franchise-seeking companies; that he guarantees to steer dubious measures through the Council, for which he demands liberal pay; that he is, in short, a successful boodler. But when there is intellect enough to get this point of view, there is also enough to make the contention that this is universally done; that all the Aldermen do it more or less successfully, but that the Alderman of the Nineteenth Ward is unique in being so generous; that such a state of affairs is to be deplored, of course, but that that is the way business is run, and we are fortunate when a kind-hearted man who is close to the people gets a large share of the boodle; that he serves these franchised companies who employ men in the building and construction of their enterprises, and that they are bound in return to give jobs to his constituency. Even when they are intelligent enough to complete the circle, and to see that the money comes, not from the pockets of the companies' agents, but from the street-car fares of people like themselves, it almost seems as if they would rather pay two cents more each time they ride than give up the consciousness that they have a big, warm-hearted friend at court who will stand by them in an emergency. The sense of just dealing comes apparently much later than the desire for protection and kindness. The Alderman is really elected because he is a good friend and neighbor.

. . . [And if we discover that men of low ideals and corrupt practice are forming popular political standards simply because such men stand by and for and with the people, then nothing remains but to obtain a like sense of identification before we can hope to modify ethical standards.]

## Lincoln Steffens

# THE SHAME OF THE CITIES

*Journalist Lincoln Steffens compiled his magazine exposés of corruption in turn-of-the-century urban America into a book,* The Shame of the Cities, *which reinforced the image of urban politics established by Bryce. However, Steffens found corruption permeating not only politics but all levels of society, and he blamed America's business mentality for lowering the nation's ethical standards. Reform, for Steffens, would not only entail attacks on the political bosses but on the corrupting businessmen as well.*

. . . Even in government we have given proofs of potential greatness, and our political failures are not complete; they are simply ridiculous. But they are ours. Not alone the triumphs and the statesmen, the defeats and the grafters also represent us, and just as truly. Why not see it so and say it?

Because, I heard, the American people won't "stand for" it. You may blame the politicians, or, indeed, any one class, but not all classes, not the people. Or you may put it on the ignorant foreign immigrant, or any one nationality, but not on all nationalities, not on the American people. But no one class is at fault, nor any one breed, nor any particular interest or group of interests. The misgovernment of the American people is misgovernment by the American people.

When I set out on my travels, an honest New Yorker told me honestly that I would find that the Irish, the Catholic Irish, were at the bottom of it all everywhere. The first city I went to was St. Louis, a German city. The next was Minneapolis, a Scandinavian city, with a leadership of New Englanders. Then came Pittsburg, Scotch Presbyterian, and that was what my New York friend was. "Ah, but they are all foreign populations," I heard. The next city was Philadelphia, the purest American community of all, and the most hopeless. And after that came Chicago and New York, both mongrel-bred, but the one a triumph of reform, the other the best example of good government that I had seen. The "foreign element" excuse is one of the hypocritical lies that save us from the clear sight of ourselves.

From Lincoln Steffens, *The Shame of the Cities* (New York, 1904), pp. 4–12, 14–16.

Another such conceit of our egotism is that which deplores our politics and lauds our business. This is the wail of the typical American citizen. Now, the typical American citizen is the business man. The typical business man is a bad citizen; he is busy. If he is a "big business man" and very busy, he does not neglect, he is busy with politics, oh, very busy and very businesslike. I found him buying boodlers in St. Louis, defending grafters in Minneapolis, originating corruption in Pittsburg, sharing with bosses in Philadelphia, deploring reform in Chicago, and beating good government with corruption funds in New York. He is a self-righteous fraud, this big business man. He is the chief source of corruption, and it were a boon if he would neglect politics. But he is not the business man that neglects politics; that worthy is the good citizen, the typical business man. He too is busy, he is the one that has no use and therefore no time for politics. When his neglect has permitted bad government to go so far that he can be stirred to action, he is unhappy, and he looks around for a cure that shall be quick, so that he may hurry back to the shop. Naturally, too, when he talks politics, he talks shop. His patent remedy is quack; it is business.

"Give us a business man," he says ("like me," he means). "Let him introduce business methods into politics and government; then I shall be left alone to attend to my business."

There is hardly an office from United States Senator down to Alderman in any part of the country to which the business man has not been elected; yet politics remains corrupt, government pretty bad, and the selfish citizen has to hold himself in readiness like the old volunteer firemen to rush forth at any hour, in any weather, to prevent the fire; and he goes out sometimes and he puts out the fire (after the damage is done) and he goes back to the shop sighing for the business man in politics. The business man has failed in politics as he has in citizenship. Why?

[Because politics is business. That's what's the matter with it. That's what's the matter with everything,—art, literature, religion, journalism, law, medicine,—they're all business, and all—as you see them.] Make politics a sport, as they do in England, or a profession, as they do in Germany, and we'll have—well, something else than we have now,—if we want it, which is another question. But don't try to reform politics with the banker, the lawyer, and the dry-goods merchant, for these are business men and there are two great hindrances to their achievement of reform: one is that they are different from, but no better than, the politicians; the other is that politics is not "their line." There are exceptions both ways. Many politicians have gone out into business and done well (Tammany ex-mayors, and nearly all the old bosses of Philadelphia are prominent financiers in their cities), and business men have gone into politics and done well (Mark Hanna, for example). They haven't reformed their adopted trades, however, though they have sometimes sharpened them most pointedly. The politician is a business man with a specialty. When a business man of some other line learns the business of politics, he is a politician, and there is not much reform left in him. Consider the United States Senate, and believe me.

The commercial spirit is the spirit of profit, not patriotism; of credit, not honor; of individual gain, not national prosperity; of trade and dickering, not principle. "My business is sacred," says the business man in his heart. "Whatever prospers my business, is good; it must be. Whatever hinders it, is wrong; it must be. A bribe is bad, that is, it is a bad thing to take; but it is not so bad to give one, not if it is necessary to my business." "Business is business" is not a political sentiment, but our politician has caught it. He takes essentially the same view of the bribe, only he saves his self-respect by piling all his contempt upon the bribe-giver, and he has the great advantage of candor. "It is wrong, maybe," he says, "but if a rich merchant can afford to do business with me for the sake of a convenience or to increase his already great wealth, I can afford, for the sake of a living, to meet him half way. I make no pretensions to virtue, not even on Sunday." And as for giving bad government or good, how about the merchant who gives bad goods or good goods, according to the demand?

But there is hope, not alone despair, in the commercialism of our politics. If our political leaders are to be always a lot of political merchants, they will supply any demand we may create. All we have to do is to establish a steady demand for good government. The boss has us split up into parties. To him parties are nothing but means to his corrupt ends. He "bolts" his party, but we must not; the bribe-giver changes his party, from one election to another, from one county to another, from one city to another, but the honest voter must not. Why? Because if the honest voter cared no more for his party than the politician and the grafter, then the honest vote would govern, and that would be bad—for graft. It is idiotic, this devotion to a machine that is used to take our sovereignty from us. If we would leave parties to the politicians, and would vote not for the party, not even for men, but for the city, and the State, and the nation, we should rule parties, and cities, and States, and nation. If we would vote in mass on the more promising ticket, or, if the two are equally bad, would throw out the party that is in, and wait till the next election and then throw out the other party that is in—then, I say, the commercial politician would feel a demand for good government and he would supply it. That process would take a generation or more to complete, for the politicians now really do not know what good government is. But it has taken as long to develop bad government, and the politicians know what that is. If it would not "go," they would offer something else, and, if the demand were steady, they, being so commercial, would "deliver the goods."

But do the people want good government? Tammany says they don't. Are the people honest? Are the people better than Tammany? Are they better than the merchant and the politician? Isn't our corrupt government, after all, representative?

President Roosevelt has been sneered at for going about the country preaching, as a cure for our American evils, good conduct in the individual, simple honesty, courage, and efficiency. "Platitudes!" the sophisticated say. Platitudes? If my observations have been true, the literal adoption of Mr. Roosevelt's reform scheme would result in a revolution, more radical and terrible to existing institutions, from the Congress to the Church, from the bank to the ward organization, than socialism or even than anarchy. Why, that would change all of us—not alone our neighbors, not alone the grafters, but you and me.

No, the contemned methods of our despised politics are the master methods of our braggart business, and the corruption that shocks us in public affairs we practice ourselves in our private concerns. There is no essential difference between the pull that gets your wife into society or a favorable review for your book, and that which gets a heeler into office, a thief out of jail, and a rich man's son on the board of directors of a corporation; none between the corruption of a labor union, a bank, and a political machine; none between a dummy director of a trust and the caucus-bound member of a legislature; none between a labor boss like Sam Parks, a boss of banks like John D. Rockefeller, a boss of railroads like J. P. Morgan, and a political boss like Matthew S. Quay. The boss is not a political, he is an American institution, the product of a freed people that have not the spirit to be free.

And it's all a moral weakness; a weakness right where we think we are strongest. Oh, we are good—on Sunday, and we are "fearfully patriotic" on the Fourth of July. But the bribe we pay to the janitor to prefer our interests to the landlord's, is the little brother of the bribe passed to the alderman to sell a city street, and the father of the air-brake stock assigned to the president of a railroad to have this life-saving invention adopted on his road. And as for graft, railroad passes, saloon and bawdy-house blackmail, and watered stock, all these belong to the same family. We are pathetically proud of our democratic institutions and our republican form of government, of our grand Constitution and our just laws. We are a free and sovereign people, we govern ourselves and the government is ours. But that is the point. We are responsible, not our leaders, since we follow them. We *let* them divert our loyalty from the United States to some "party"; we *let* them boss the party and turn our municipal democracies into autocracies and our republican nation into a plutocracy. We cheat our government and we let our leaders loot it, and we let them wheedle and bribe our sovereignty from us. True, they pass for us strict laws, but we are content to let them pass also bad laws, giving away public property in exchange; and our good, and often impossible, laws we allow to be used for oppression and blackmail. And what can we say? We break our own laws and rob our own government, the lady at the custom-house, the lyncher with his rope, and the captain of industry with his bribe and his rebate. The spirit of graft and of lawlessness is the American spirit.

*          *          *

The people are not innocent. That is the only "news" in all the journalism of these articles, and no doubt that was not new to many observers. It was to me. When I set out to describe the corrupt systems of certain typical cities, I meant to show simply how the people were deceived and betrayed. But in the very first study— St. Louis—the startling truth lay bare that corruption was not merely political; it was financial, commercial, social; the ramifications of boodle were so complex, various, and far-reaching, that one mind could hardly grasp them, and not even Joseph W. Folk, the tireless prosecutor, could follow them all. This state of things was indicated in the first article which Claude H. Wetmore and I compiled together, but it was not shown plainly enough. Mr. Wetmore lived in St. Louis, and he had respect for names which meant little to me. But when I went next to Minneapolis alone, I could see more independently, without respect for persons, and there were traces of the same phenomenon. The first St. Louis article was called "Tweed Days in St. Louis," and though the "better citizen" received attention the Tweeds were the center of interest. In "The Shame of Minneapolis," the truth was put into the title; it was the Shame of Minneapolis; not of the Ames administration, not of the Tweeds, but of the city and its citizens. And yet Minneapolis was not nearly so bad as St. Louis; police graft is never so universal as boodle. It is more shocking, but it is so filthy that it cannot involve so large a part of society. So I returned to St. Louis, and I went over the whole ground again, with the people in mind, not alone the caught and convicted boodlers. And this time the true meaning of "Tweed days in St. Louis" was made plain. The article was called "The Shamelessness of St. Louis," and that was the burden of the story. In Pittsburg also the people was the subject, and though the civic spirit there was better, the extent of the corruption throughout the social organization of the community was indicated. But it was not till I got to Philadelphia that the possibilities of popular corruption were worked out to the limit of humiliating confession. That was the place for such a study. There is nothing like it in the country, except possibly, in Cincinnati. Philadelphia certainly is not merely corrupt, but corrupted, and this was made clear. Philadelphia was charged up to—the American citizen.

It was impossible in the space of a magazine article to cover in any one city all the phases of municipal government, so I chose cities that typified most strikingly some particular phase or phases. Thus as St. Louis exemplified boodle; Minneapolis, police graft; Pittsburg, a political and industrial machine; and Philadelphia, general civic corruption; so Chicago was an illustration of reform, and New York of good government. All these things occur in most of these places. There are, and long have been, reformers in St. Louis, and there is to-day police graft there. Minneapolis has had boodling and council reform, and boodling is breaking out there again. Pittsburg has general corruption, and Philadelphia a very perfect political machine. Chicago has police graft and a low order of administrative and general corruption which permeates business, labor, and society generally. As for New York, the metropolis might exemplify almost anything that occurs anywhere in American cities, but no city has had for many years such a good administration as was that of Mayor Seth Low.

*George Washington Plunkitt*
# BOSSES PRESERVE THE NATION

*The old Tammany ward boss George Washington Plunkitt was active in New York politics from the time of Boss Tweed to the early years of the twentieth century. Throughout his career, he "seen his opportunities" and took them, tying his fortunes to Tammany Bosses Tweed, Kelly, Croker, and Murphy. His harbor transportation and general contracting business, in conjunction with his political connections and attitude toward "honest graft," brought Plunkitt great wealth. In 1905, William L. Riordon, a political reporter for the old* New York Post, *published* Plunkitt of Tammany Hall, *a collection of talks he allegedly had with the ward boss. The collection makes evident Plunkitt's fondness for machine politics and his belief that "bosses preserve the nation."*

"When I retired from the Senate, I thought I would take a good, long rest, such a rest as a man needs who has held office for about forty years, and has held four different offices in one year and

From William L. Riordon, *Plunkitt of Tammany Hall* (New York, 1905), pp. 150–155.

drawn salaries from three of them at the same time. Drawin' so many salaries is rather fatiguin', you know, and, as I said, I started out for a rest; but when I seen how things were goin' in New York State, and how a great big black shadow hung over us, I said to myself: 'No rest for you, George. Your work ain't done. Your country still needs you and you mustn't lay down yet.'

"What was the great big black shadow? It was the primary election law, amended so as to knock out what are called the party bosses by lettin' in everybody at the primaries and givin' control over them to state officials. Oh, yes, that is a good way to do up the so-called bosses, but, have you ever thought what would become of the country if the bosses were put out of business, and their places were taken by a lot of cart-tail orators and college graduates? It would mean chaos. It would be just like takin' a lot of dry-goods clerks and settin' them to run express trains on the New York Central Railroad. It makes my heart bleed to think of it. Ignorant people are always talkin' against party bosses, but just wait till the bosses are gone! Then, and not until then, will they get the right sort of epitaphs, as Patrick Henry or Robert Emmet said.

"Look at the bosses of Tammany Hall in the last twenty years. What magnificent men! To them New York City owes pretty much all it is to-day. John Kelly, Richard Croker, and Charles F. Murphy —what names in American history compares with them, except Washington and Lincoln? They built up the grand Tammany organization, and the organization built up New York. Suppose the city had to depend for the last twenty years on irresponsible concerns like the Citizens' Union, where would it be now? You can make a pretty good guess if you recall the Strong and Low administrations when there was no boss, and the heads of departments were at odds all the time with each other, and the Mayor was at odds with the lot of them. They spent so much time in arguin' and makin' grand-stand play, that the interests of the city were forgotten. Another administration of that kind would put New York back a quarter of a century.

"Then see how beautiful a Tammany city government runs, with a so-called boss directin' the whole shootin' match! The machinery moves so noiseless that you wouldn't think there was any. If there's any differences of opinion, the Tammany leader settles them quietly, and his orders go every time. How nice it is for the people to feel that they can get up in the mornin' without bein' afraid of seein' in the papers that the Commissioner of Water Supply has sandbagged the Dock Commissioner, and that the Mayor and heads of the departments have been taken to the police court as witnesses! That's no joke. I remember that, under Strong, some commissioners came very near sandbaggin' one another.

"Of course, the newspapers like the reform administration. Why? Because these administrations, with their daily rows, furnish as racy news as prize-fights or divorce cases. Tammany don't care to get in the papers. It goes right along attendin' to business quietly and only wants to be let alone. That's one reason why the papers are against us.

"Some papers complain that the bosses get rich while devotin' their lives to the interests of the city. What of it? If opportunities for turnin' an honest dollar comes their way, why shouldn't they take advantage of them, just as I have done? As I said, in another talk, there is honest graft and dishonest graft. The bosses go in for the former. There is so much of it in this big town that they would be fools to go in for dishonest graft.

"Now, the primary election law threatens to do away with the boss and make the city government a menagerie. That's why I can't take the rest I counted on. I'm goin' to propose a bill for the next session of the legislature repealin' this dangerous law, and leavin' the primaries entirely to the organizations themselves, as they used to be. Then will return the good old times, when our district leaders could have nice comfortable primary elections at some place selected by themselves and let in only men that they approved of as good Democrats. Who is a better judge of the Democracy of a man who offers his vote than the leader of the district? Who is better equipped to keep out undesirable voters?

"The men who put through the primary law are the same crowd that stand for the civil service blight and they have the same objects in view—the destruction of governments by party, the downfall of the constitution and hell generally."

# II THE MACHINE AND ITS FUNCTIONS

Robert K. Merton

# THE LATENT FUNCTIONS OF THE MACHINE

*Rejecting a moral evaluation of the political machine, sociologist Robert K. Merton points out that it fulfilled functions inadequately carried out by the official institutions of local urban government. While constitutional and other limitations dispersed and restricted governmental power, the boss and his machine centralized authority and decision-making. At a price, they got things done for those in need. The student should consider, in the light of the latent functions of the machine, whether the social costs of corruption were repaid in services and benefits to society. Professor Merton is author of* Social Theory and Social Structure *and other sociological works.*

Since moral evaluations in a society tend to be largely in terms of the manifest consequences of a practice or code, we should be prepared to find that analysis in terms of latent functions at times run counter to prevailing moral evaluations. For it does not follow that the latent functions will operate in the same fashion as the manifest consequences which are ordinarily the basis of these judgments. Thus, in larger sectors of the American population, the political machine or the "political racket" are judged as unequivocally "bad" and "undesirable." The grounds for such moral judgment vary somewhat, but they consist substantially in pointing out that political machines violate moral codes: political patronage violates the code of selecting personnel on the basis of impersonal qualifications rather than on grounds of party loyalty or contributions to the party war-chest; bossism violates the code that votes should be based on individual appraisal of the qualifications of candidates and of political issues, and not on abiding loyalty to a feudal leader; bribery and "honest graft" obviously offend the proprieties of property; "protection" for crime clearly violates the law and the mores; and so on.

In view of these manifold respects in which political machines, in varying degrees, run counter to the mores and at times to the law, it becomes pertinent to inquire how they manage to continue in operation. The familiar "explanations" for the continuance of the political machine are not here in point. To be sure, it may well be that if "respectable citizenry" would carry through their political obligations, if the electorate were to be alert and enlightened; if the number of elective officers were substantially reduced from the dozens, even hundreds, which the average voter is now expected to appraise in the course of local, county, state and national elections, if the electorate were activated by the "wealthy and educated classes without whose participation," as the not-always democratically oriented Bryce put it, "the best-framed government must speedily degenerate," if these and a plethora of similar changes in political structure were introduced, perhaps the "evils" of the political machine would indeed be exorcized. But it should be noted that these changes are not typically introduced, that political machines have the phoenix-like quality of arising strong and unspoiled from their ashes, that, in short, this structure exhibits a notable vitality in many areas of American political life.

Proceeding from the functional view, therefore, that we should *ordinarily* (not invariably) expect persistent social patterns and social structures to perform positive functions *which are at the time not adequately fulfilled by other existing patterns and structures,* the thought occurs that perhaps this publicly maligned organization is, *under present conditions,* satisfying basic latent functions. A brief examination of current analyses of this type of structure may also serve to illustrate additional problems of functional analysis.

## Some Functions of the Political Machine

Without presuming to enter into the variations of detail marking different political machines—a Tweed, Vare, Crump, Flynn, Hague are by no means identical types of bosses—we can briefly examine the functions more or less common to the political machine, as a generic type of social organization. We neither attempt to itemize all the diverse functions of the political machine nor imply that all these functions are similarly fulfilled by each and every machine.

The key structural function of the Boss is to organize, centralize and maintain in good working condition "the scattered fragments of power" which are at present dispersed through our political organization. By this centralized organization of political power,

the boss and his apparatus can satisfy the needs of diverse subgroups in the larger community which are not adequately satisfied
by legally devised and culturally approved social structures.

To understand the role of bossism and the machine, therefore,
we must look at two types of sociological variables: (1) the *struc-*
*tural context* which makes it difficult, if not impossible, for morally
approved structures to fulfill essential social functions, thus leaving
the door open for political machines (or their structural equivalents)
to fulfill these functions and (2) the subgroups whose distinctive
needs are left unsatisfied, except for the latent functions which the
machine in fact fulfills.

## Structural Context

The constitutional framework of American political organization
specifically precludes the legal possibility of highly centralized
power and, it has been noted, thus "discourages the growth of
effective and responsible leadership. The framers of the Constitution,
as Woodrow Wilson observed, set up the check and balance system
'to keep government at a sort of mechanical equipoise by means
of a standing amicable contest among its several organic parts.'
They distrusted power as dangerous to liberty: and therefore they
spread it thin and erected barriers against its concentration." This
dispersion of power is found not only at the national level but in
local areas as well. "As a consequence," Sait goes on to observe,
"when *the people or particular groups* among them demanded
positive action, no one had adequate authority to act. The machine
provided an antidote."

[The constitutional dispersion of power not only makes for difficulty of effective decision and action but when action does occur
it is defined and hemmed in by legalistic considerations.] In consequence, there develops "a much *more human system* of partisan
government, whose chief object soon became the circumvention of
government by law. . . . The lawlessness of the extra-official
democracy was merely the counterpoise of the legalism of the official
democracy. The lawyer having been permitted to subordinate
democracy to the Law, the Boss had to be called in to extricate the
victim, which he did after a fashion and for a consideration."

Officially, political power is dispersed. Various well-known expedients were devised for this manifest objective. Not only was there the familiar separation of powers among the several branches of the government but, in some measure, tenure in each office was limited, rotation in office approved. And the scope of power inherent in each office was severely circumscribed. Yet, observes Sait in rigorously functional terms, "Leadership is necessary; and *since* it does not develop readily within the constitutional framework, the Boss provides it in a crude and irresponsible form from the outside."

Put in more generalized terms, *the functional deficiencies of the official structure generate an alternative (unofficial) structure to fulfill existing needs somewhat more effectively.* Whatever its specific historical origins, the political machine persists as an apparatus for satisfying otherwise unfulfilled needs of diverse groups in the population. By turning to a few of these subgroups and their characteristic needs, we shall be led at once to a range of latent functions of the political machine.

## Functions of the Political Machine for Diverse Subgroups

It is well known that one source of strength of the political machine derives from its roots in the local community and the neighborhood. The political machine does not regard the electorate as a vague, undifferentiated mass of voters. With a keen sociological intuition, the machine recognizes that the voter is primarily a man living in a specific neighborhood, with specific personal problems and personal wants. Public issues are abstract and remote; private problems are extremely concrete and immediate. It is not through the generalized appeal to large public concerns that the machine operates, but through the direct, quasi-feudal relationships between local representatives of the machine and voters in their neighborhood. Elections are won in the precinct.

The machine welds its link with ordinary men and women by elaborate networks of personal relations. Politics is transformed into personal ties. The precinct captain "must be a friend to every man, assuming if he does not feel sympathy with the unfortunate, and utilizing in his good works the resources which the boss puts at his disposal." The precinct captain is forever a friend in need. In our prevailingly impersonal society, the machine, through its local agents, fulfills the important social *function of humanizing*

*and personalizing all manner of assistance* to those in need.⌋ Food-
baskets and jobs, legal and extra-legal advice, setting to rights
minor scrapes with the law, helping the bright poor boy to a political
scholarship in a local college, looking after the bereaved—the
whole range of crises when a feller needs a friend, and, above
all, a friend who knows the score and who can do something about
it,—all these find the ever-helpful precinct captain available in the
pinch.

⌈To assess this function of the political machine adequately, it is
important to note not only the fact that aid *is* provided but *the
manner in which it is provided.*⌋After all, other agencies do exist for
dispensing such assistance. Welfare agencies, settlement houses,
legal aid clinics, medical aid in free hospitals, public relief departments, immigration authorities—these and a multitude of other
organizations are available to provide the most varied types of
assistance. But in contrast to the professional techniques of the
welfare worker which may typically represent in the mind of the
recipient the cold, bureaucratic dispensation of limited aid following
upon detailed investigation of *legal* claims to aid of the "client," are
the unprofessional techniques of the precinct captain who asks no
questions, exacts no compliance with legal rules of eligibility and
does not "snoop" into private affairs.

⌈For many, the loss of "self-respect" is too high a price for legal-
ized assistance.⌋ In contrast to the gulf between the settlement
house workers who so often come from a different social class,
educational background and ethnic group, the precinct worker is
"just one of us," who understands what it's all about. The condescending lady bountiful can hardly compete with the understanding friend in need. In *this struggle between alternative structures for
fulfilling the nominally same function* of providing aid and support to
those who need it, it is clearly the machine politician who is better
integrated with the groups which he serves than the impersonal,
professionalized, socially distant and legally constrained welfare
worker. And since the politician can at times influence and manipulate the official organizations for the dispensation of assistance,
whereas the welfare worker has practically no influence on the
political machine, this only adds to his greater effectiveness. More
colloquially and also, perhaps, more incisively, it was the Boston

ward-leader, Martin Lomasny, who described this essential function to the curious Lincoln Steffens: "I think," said Lomasny, "that there's got to be in every ward somebody that any bloke can come to—no matter what he's done—and get help. *Help, you understand; none of your law and justice, but help.*"

The "deprived classes," then, constitute one subgroup for whom the political machine clearly satisfies wants not adequately satisfied in the same fashion by the legitimate social structure.

For a second subgroup, that of business (primarily "big" business but also "small") the political boss serves the function of providing those political privileges which entail immediate economic gains. Business corporations, among which the public utilities (railroads, local transportation companies, communications corporations, electric light) are simply the most conspicuous in this regard, seek special political dispensations which will enable them to stabilize their situation and to near their objective of maximizing profits. Interestingly enough, corporations often want to avoid a chaos of uncontrolled competition. They want the greater security of an economic czar who controls, regulates and organizes competition, providing this czar is not a public official with his decisions subject to public scrutiny and public control. (The latter would be "government control," and hence taboo.) The political boss fulfills these requirements admirably.

Examined for a moment apart from any "moral" considerations, the political apparatus of the Boss is effectively designed to perform these functions with a minimum of inefficiency. Holding the strings of diverse governmental divisions, bureaus and agencies in his competent hands, the Boss rationalizes the relations between public and private business. He serves as the business community's ambassador in the otherwise alien (and sometimes unfriendly) realm of government. And, in strict business-like terms, he is well-paid for his economic services to his respectable business clients. In an article entitled, "An Apology to Graft," Steffens suggested that "Our economic system, which held up riches, power and acclaim as prizes to men bold enough and able enough to buy corruptly timber, mines, oil fields and franchises and 'get away with it,' was at fault." And, in a conference with a hundred or so of Los Angeles business leaders, he described a fact well known to all of them: the Boss and his machine were an *integral part* of the organization of the economy. "You cannot build or operate a railroad, or a street railway, gas, water, or power company, develop and operate a mine, or get forests and cut timber on a large scale, or run any privileged business, without corrupting or joining in the corruption of the government. You tell me privately that you must, and here I am telling you semipublicly that you must. And that is so all over the country. And that means that we have an organization of society in which, *for some reason,* you and your kind, the ablest, most intelligent, most imaginative, daring, and resourceful leaders of society, are and must be against society and its laws and its all-around growth."

[Since the demand for the services of special privileges are built into the structure of the society, the Boss fulfills diverse functions for this second subgroup of business-seeking-privilege.] These "needs" of business, as presently constituted, are not adequately provided for by "conventional" and "culturally approved" social structures; consequently, the extra-legal but more-or-less efficient organization of the political machine comes to provide these services. To adopt an *exclusively* moral attitude toward the "corrupt political machine" is to lose sight of the very structural conditions which generate the "evil" that is so bitterly attacked. To adopt a functional outlook on the political machine is not to provide an apologia, but a more solid base for modifying or eliminating the machine, *providing* specific structural arrangements are introduced either for eliminating these effective demands of the business community or, if that is the objective, of satisfying these demands through alternative means.

[A third set of distinctive functions fulfilled by the political machine for a special subgroup is that of providing alternative channels of social mobility for those otherwise excluded from the more conventional avenues for personal "advancement."] Both the sources of this special "need" (for social mobility) and the respect in which the political machine comes to help satisfy this need can be understood by examining the structure of the larger culture and society. As is well known, the American culture lays enormous emphasis on money and power as a "success" goal legitimate for all members of the society. By no means alone in our inventory of cultural goals, it still remains among the most heavily endowed with positive affect and value. However, certain subgroups and certain ecological areas are notable for the relative absence of opportunity for achieving these (monetary and power) types of success. They constitute, in short, sub-populations where "the cultural emphasis upon pecuniary success has been absorbed, but where there is *little access to conventional and legitimate* means for attaining such success. The conventional occupational opportunities of persons in (such areas) are almost completely limited to manual labor. Given our cultural stigmatization of manual labor, and its correlate, the prestige of white-collar work," it is clear that the result is a tendency to achieve these culturally approved objectives *through whatever means are possible.* These people are on the one hand "asked to orient their conduct toward the prospect of accumulating wealth [and power] and, on the other, they are largely denied effective opportunities to do so institutionally."

It is within this context of social structure that the political machine fulfills the basic function of providing avenues of social mobility for the otherwise disadvantaged. Within this context, even the corrupt political machine and the racket "represent the triumph of amoral intelligence over morally prescribed 'failure' when the channels of vertical mobility are closed or narrowed *in a society which places a high premium on economic affluence,* [*power*] *and social ascent for all its members.".* . .

This, then represents a third type of function performed for a distinctive subgroup. [This function, it may be noted in passing, is fulfilled by the *sheer* existence and operation of the political machine, for it is in the machine itself that these individuals and subgroups find their culturally induced needs more or less satisfied.] It refers to the services which the political apparatus provides for its own personnel. But seen in the wider social context we have set forth, it no longer appears as *merely* a means of self-aggrandizement for profit-hungry and power-hungry *individuals,* but as an organized provision for *subgroups* otherwise excluded or restricted from the race for "getting ahead."

Just as the political machine performs services for "legitimate" business, so it operates to perform not dissimilar services for "illegitimate" business: vice, crime and rackets. Once again, the basic sociological role of the machine in this respect can be more fully appreciated only if one temporarily abandons attitudes of moral indignation, to examine with all moral innocence the actual workings of the organization. In this light, it at once appears that the subgroup of the professional criminal, racketeer, gambler, has basic similarities of organization, demands and operation to the subgroup of the industrialist, man of business, speculator. If there is a Lumber King or an Oil King, there is also a Vice King or a Racket King. If expansive legitimate business organizes administrative and financial syndicates to "rationalize" and to "integrate" diverse areas of production and business enterprise, so expansive rackets and crime organize syndicates to bring order to the otherwise chaotic areas of production of illicit goods and services. If legitimate business regards the proliferation of small business enterprises as wasteful and inefficient, substituting, for example, the giant chain stores for the hundreds of corner groceries, so illegitimate business adopts the same businesslike attitude, and syndicates crime and vice.

Finally, and in many respects, most important, is the basic similarity, if not near-identity, of the economic role of "legitimate" business and "illegitimate" business. *Both are in some degree concerned with the provision of goods and services for which there is an economic demand.* Morals aside, they are both business, industrial and professional enterprises, dispensing goods and services which some people want, for which there is a market in which goods and services are transformed into commodities. And, in a prevalently market society, we should expect appropriate enterprises to arise whenever there is a market demand for given goods or services.

*       *       *

The distinctive function of the political machine for their criminal, vice and racket clientele is to enable them to operate in satisfying the economic demands of a large market without due interference from the government. Just as big business may contribute funds to the political party war-chest to ensure a minimum of governmental interference, so with big rackets and big crime. In both instances, the political machine can, in varying degrees, provide "protection." In both instances, many features of the structural context are identical: (1) market demands for goods and services; (2) the operators' concern with maximizing gains from their enterprises; (3) the need for partial control of government which might otherwise interfere with these activities of businessmen; (4) the need for an efficient, powerful and centralized agency to provide an effective liaison of "business" with government.

Without assuming that the foregoing pages exhaust either the range of functions or the range of subgroups served by the political machine, we can at least see that *it presently fulfills some functions for these diverse subgroups which are not adequately fulfilled by culturally approved or more conventional structures.*

Several additional implications of the functional analysis of the political machine can be mentioned here only in passing, although they obviously require to be developed at length. First, the foregoing analysis has direct implications for *social engineering.* It helps explain why the periodic efforts at "political reform," "turning the rascals out" and "cleaning political house" are typically short-lived and ineffectual. It exemplifies a basic theorem: *any attempt to eliminate an existing social structure without providing adequate alternative structures for fulfilling the functions previously fulfilled by the abolished organization is doomed to failure.* (Needless to say, this theorem has much wider bearing than the one instance of the political machine.) When "political reform" confines itself to the manifest task of "turning the rascals out," it is engaging in little more than sociological magic. The reform may for a time bring new figures into the political limelight; it may serve the casual social function of re-assuring the electorate that the moral virtues remain intact and will ultimately triumph; it may actually effect a turnover in the personnel of the political machine; it may even, for a time, so curb the activities of the machine as to leave unsatisfied the many needs it has previously fulfilled. But, inevitably, unless the reform also involves a "re-forming" of the social and political structure such that the existing needs are satisfied by alternative structures or unless it involves a change which eliminates these needs altogether, the political machine will return to its integral place in the social scheme of things. *To seek social change, without due recognition of the manifest and latent functions performed by the social organization undergoing change, is to indulge in social ritual rather than social engineering.* The concepts of manifest and latent functions (or their equivalents) are indispensable elements in the theoretic repertoire of the social engineer. In this crucial sense, these concepts are not "merely" theoretical (in the abusive sense of the term), but are eminently practical. In the deliberate enactment of social change, they can be ignored only at the price of considerably heightening the risk of failure.

A second implication of our analysis of the political machine also has a bearing upon areas wider than the one we have considered. The "paradox" has often been noted that the supporters of the political machine include both the "respectable" business class elements who are, of course, opposed to the criminal or racketeer and the distinctly "unrespectable" elements of the underworld. And, at first appearance, this is cited as an instance of very strange bedfellows. The learned judge is not infrequently called upon to sentence the very racketeer beside whom he sat the night before at an informal dinner of the political bigwigs. The district attorney jostles the exonerated convict on his way to the back room where the Boss has called a meeting. The big business man may complain almost as bitterly as the big racketeer about the "extortionate" contributions to the party fund demanded by the Boss. Social opposites meet—in the smoke-filled room of the successful politician.

In the light of a functional analysis all this of course no longer seems paradoxical. Since the machine serves both the businessman and the criminal man, the two seemingly antipodal groups intersect. This points to a more general theorem: *the social functions of an organization help determine the structure (including the recruitment of personnel involved in the structure), just as the structure helps determine the effectiveness with which the functions are fulfilled.* In terms of social status, the business group and the criminal group are indeed poles apart. But status does not fully determine behavior and the inter-relations between groups. Functions modify these relations. Given their distinctive needs, the several subgroups in the large society are "integrated," whatever their personal desires or intentions, by the centralizing structure which serves these several needs. In a phrase with many implications which require further study, *structure affects function and function affects structure.*

## Eric L. McKitrick
# THE STUDY OF CORRUPTION

*In "The Study of Corruption," historian Eric McKitrick uses Merton's suppositions as a base, but goes on to ask how, if at all, the sociologist's pattern of machine politics has changed since the Progressive era. For McKitrick, the machine is a dynamic, changing organism; in the selection which follows he explains the evolution of boss politics during the twentieth century. Professor McKitrick has authored* Andrew Johnson and Reconstruction *and several articles on various aspects of American history.*

An important thing to note with regard to the Merton scheme is that it seems to have been postulated for what might be called a "classical" period in the history of American machine politics. The most perceptive field work ever done in this area is still probably that of Lincoln Steffens—and since it is from Steffens that Mr. Merton has taken his major cues, it is inevitable that the balance and arrangement of his categories should be most appropriate to a state of things which existed about fifty years ago: a period roughly centering on the year 1905.

This is not meant to intimate that the model does not apply today. It is valid and accurate in all its major details. It is so set up that any alterations in it would have to be more in the nature of refinements than of basic changes. But the subject matter itself has changed in a great many ways since Steffens' time, and I emphasize this in order to make my key point. In the absence of outside stimuli—such as a general public interest in "reform" (or, for that matter, a primary *need* for reform)—pressure for new work and new insights will have to come from somewhere within the social sciences, and, specifically, I would say that it will have to come from the field of American history. Its raw data will be found in the form of substantial materials which must now be called "historical": material covering the period in which our cities underwent their most phenomenal phases of growth—material which dates back at least to the end of the Civil War. Any theoretical model for the explanation of social phenomena has a tendency, in spite of

From Eric L. McKitrick, "The Study of Corruption," *Political Science Quarterly* (December 1957), pp. 502–514. Reprinted by permission of the author.

all precautions, to be static. But if there is anything about our social scene that is insistently dynamic, it is the tempo of our political life—and to get the sense of dynamism in political structures (that is, *change, and the things that produce it), one needs the sense of time.* We know a great deal about the functions of such structures at given points in time. But of equal, if not greater, importance to political sociology today is the course of transformation which these structures—these "machines"—have undergone over the past two generations. This is now what makes "history" such a vital dimension. An understanding of such change, and of the reasons for it, is bound to "feed back" into one's understanding and judgment of the very functions themselves. . . .

. . . To what extent does [Merton's pattern] hold today? It is a pattern whose formal outlines are still in some way to be recognized in all our major cities. However, the specific activities and operations represented by these formal categories have been so immeasurably altered and transformed as to change the very *symmetry* of the pattern, and to raise certain very crucial questions. Has the old system for practical purposes (as some writers have begun to assert) really "broken down"? Or does it continue to operate within a more limited area? What has been the effect of the reform tradition? Has the boss "gone straight"? What kinds of loyalties can the machine command today? What kinds of things can it still do—and are there things that it can no longer do?

Certain kinds of historical problems immediately suggest themselves—problems having to do with the *persistence* of the "corrupt machine." For instance: under what conditions has it been possible for a reform movement to be successful? We find that it has never quite been a matter of civic affairs reaching a given point of "rottenness," with the honest citizens at that point making common cause to strike down the machine. What seems to have been required, as a matter of historical experience, is the combining of other factors, fairly complex and not always easy to identify. Such factors include points at which the machine has ceased to serve its clients responsibly—points at which services could no longer be considered worth the prices asked. The arrival of hard times could quickly precipitate such a situation. An even more sensitive point could be the one at which (for whatever reason) the machine's internal solidarity had become weakened—because of power struggles, some temporary loss of internal responsibility, perhaps a weakening of loyalties resulting from inequitable distribution of spoils. Variations on these themes will be found, if one is looking for them, recurring again and again in the literature. They are admirably spelled out in the downfall of the Tweed machine. Here we see the Boss having lost all bearings, all sense of proportion, launching a series of insane depredations, and alienating his followers by refusing to distribute the loot honorably. The Ring had become virtually a *personal* operation, with Tweed's raids upon the city treasury far exceeding what could reasonably be afforded. Here, moreover, we see the critical increment of reform energy coming from *within:* Samuel Tilden's success was in large measure due to strategic assistance from the Tammany organization, and to the invaluable inside knowledge which was the product of having himself worked, for years, with Tammany Hall.

A situation of this sort may undoubtedly be matched by numerous others—and, in fact, by still others turned, as it were, inside out. For, conversely, it may be assumed that a reform government which offers nothing as a substitute for the functions performed by the machine will find itself very shortly in a state of paralysis. The mayoralty of Seth Low in New York in the early 1900s furnishes such a case; another is found in the efforts of Joseph Folk to "reform" St. Louis in 1902; and numerous others may be located all through the reform annals of the Progressive Era.

Such might be called the "functional" approach on the simplest and most straightforward plane. But it leads into parallel problems of even greater interest and greater subtlety. Take this question: what is the function of the reform movement—not for destroying the machine but for reinvigorating it, for renewing its vitality, for *helping* it to persist? At this point the "machine" metaphor itself becomes misleading. It has in no case, apparently, been a thing that could be smashed in the way that an engine can be rendered useless by the destruction of a few key parts. Rather, its very complexity, the very functional autonomy of so many of its parts, makes it more like an *organism*. For instance, solidarity at the ward level seems to persist almost by habit: Plunkitt of Tammany Hall—then a ward leader—survived the destruction of Tweed and flourished, and his experience must have been reënacted by many another in comparable circumstances. How might this be explained?

Taking this situation as the focal point for a whole range of problems, one might attempt to picture the scene at local head-quarters the day after an election in which smashing victories had been won by the reform ticket. One may picture the post-mortem (a proceeding built into American politics): it would most surely include a highly critical reappraisal of the power situation in the ward—and those present would be the first to understand why the organization had lost. A further result would compare very closely with Durkheim's analysis of what happens at funerals: a ritual re-affirmation of group solidarity. Still another consequence would be that the demands normally made on the machine would (in view of lean times to come) tend to drop off. Therefore—assuming that the lean period did not last too long—it might be predicted that the aftermath of defeat would coincide with precisely that phase of the machine's greatest moral solidarity. Some highly interesting con-clusions might be expected to flow from this. Granting any other functions remaining for the machine to perform—and by definition they always exist—might not these be precisely the conditions in which they would be discovered? A crude example is afforded by the breakup of the Whisky Ring in Grant's time; the "army of termites" (as Matthew Josephson put it) promptly marched into the Post Office Department. Or, let the setting be a little less extreme and more refined: such conditions as those just described might simply serve as a test for activities whose *style* must be altered from time to time in order to remain acceptable. Boss Kelly of Chi-cago, according to legend, was always pleased to have Paul Douglas somewhere on the scene; his use of Douglas was as a standing threat to "any of the boys who got too hungry." A final point to be made along these lines is that the very informal nature of the ma-chine will set limits at *any* time upon its stability—which would mean that its internal leadership must remain aggressive and dy-namic to keep from being unhorsed by disaffected henchmen. The most natural alliance that an insurgent group could reach for would be an alliance with reformers. Other factions standing by could then, like Lord Stanley on Bosworth field, take their choice. The machine, in other words, has been anything but a torpid institution: a perennial state of internal "yeastiness" has made it a dynamic one.

Another set of problems, in which historical analysis and the use of historical materials are indispensable, would have to do with *long-term* changes in the entire system of machine rule. Here the reform tradition must be given its due in another way, for the very process of evolution in civic politics has been accompanied by reform groups taking up the slack and calling the turn as change occurs. The city manager and city commission plans never quite produced—in themselves—the effects hoped for by their early exponents, but they may still be considered as symptoms of a long-term process whose tendency has been toward ever-continued extension, rationalization and stabilization of official administrative agencies. Probably the most specific and most important single expression of this has been the extension of civil service into municipal government. Today, for example, a considerable sector of Tammany's former patronage preserves in New York City is blanketed by a very efficient system of civil service.

The notion of evolutionary change could be carried directly into the specific functions enumerated in Mr. Merton's conceptual scheme. Upon the welfare functions, for instance, time has unquestionably left its mark. Here, a considerable number of the services once performed for unassimilated immigrant groups and for the economically underprivileged are today no longer needed. The need has been eroded away by the assimilation process itself, by the development of scientific welfare on municipal and state-federal levels, and, most especially, by a relatively long period of full-employment capitalism. The result has been mobility, a constant turnover of population in urban areas—all of which has been deeply subversive of neighborhood solidarity. Or, take those functions performed for legitimate business. If it is kept in mind that the protection, the controls, and the umpiring have been "*un*official," as opposed to "official," there can be little doubt as to which direction the curve has gone over time, since one of the most dramatic features of our political history since 1933 has been the extension of official public controls into every aspect of business and over all kinds of businesses. Such change is, of course, anything but absolute; the old pattern, in some form, is still there. I am only indicating what the time dimension has been doing to it.

The most fascinating changes of all, and by far the most complex and difficult to trace down, are those connected with Mr. Merton's other two functions—the functions involving social mobility and relationships with the underworld. One of the most remarkable of recent discoveries in the social sciences has been the manner in which these two areas are related—the manner in which (whether the political machine is directly involved or not) they grade into one another. Somewhere along the way a conceptual block has been removed, and we are now able to see that not only do the values of mobility, status and respectability operate in the underworld in a way precisely analogous to their workings in the "upperworld," but also, that the extent to which the two worlds *overlap* in shared values is considerable. All of this furnishes us a final set of problems directly related to those already touched upon.

In drawing a pattern of corruption (loosely used here as a generic term for covering a wide variety of things) might it not be possible to trace not only the obvious shifts and transformations but also a pattern of *energy*? What happens when obstacles are placed in a particular area of corruption? Is the result an alternative pattern? Perhaps—but what about the stabilization of *existing* patterns? The same question could be put in another way—in terms of the social-mobility function (either in politics or the underworld) for socially deprived ethnic groups. Is there a possible correlation between the rise to social acceptability and the stabilization of particular forms of corruption in which members of these groups have specialized? Might not the very high value which American society at large sets upon mobility serve over time as a built-in check—as a stimulus for (say) "cleaning up" the rackets? This surely goes back at least to the days of Plunkitt—he was the man who made the virtuous distinction between "honest" and "dishonest" graft.

The Italian community of a generation ago may provide the clue to the way the mechanism works. Assume at the outset a series of status gradations all the way up through narcotics, prostitution, and ultimately gambling—and in which the gamblers would be, as it were, the "gentlemen." Costello would handle the gambling,

Luciano the girls and dope. Now what has, in fact, happened between then and today? As the entire Italian community has moved up, the higher-status brackets of the underworld have apparently come under tremendous crowding and pressure (gambling at large having become almost respectable), whereas the lower grades have been vacated to unorganized riffraff. No one of comparable prestige has arisen to fill the shoes of Lucky Luciano, and probably no one will. Moving up, then, into politics, we see the New York civic scene today liberally dotted with substantial citizens of Italian origin. Indeed, it appears that the same mechanism just described (simple mobility—with or without an "ethnic" dimension) has been at work within Tammany Hall itself. One of Mr. DeSapio's current problems seems to be the presence of significant numbers of liberal, civic-conscious young people working in the local clubs simply for the fun of it. The "Boss" is not finding it easy to give away what patronage he has, since the very people to be rewarded are turning out to be better placed elsewhere, in business and in the professions.

Let me now return to my original point. I would like to repeat my belief that those studies which can most appropriately embrace the kinds of questions I have raised will come more and more to have a historical framework. An excellent type of investigation, simple in format but with the flexibility needed for moving into any number of related areas, would be the life-study of a machine. Here, with the historical dimension, one could get the very crucial sense of a *cycle*. For cycles are long, and they embrace much change. One might further predict that the historian to whom this kind of project will be of interest will tend more and more to come into it equipped with analytical tools which he has appropriated from elsewhere but domesticated for his own special requirements. They may not ease his task, but they will make him sensitive to a whole range of vital connections which, admittedly, past historical studies (and many "scientific" ones as well) have left untouched.

I cannot resist a final question. Is the machine headed for extinction? Is it getting "cleaner and cleaner"? Conceivably not—not necessarily. New predictions could very well center on a new mobility-cycle for ethnic groups still not yet "arrived"; and this might involve a period of renewed machine activity in which the tone of politics could once more drop quite noticeably. For instance, what might happen when municipal patronage and civil service jobs are no longer attractive to (say) bright young Jewish and Italian lawyers —no longer within their dignity? One clear sign of rising mobility among Negro and Puerto Rican groups would be the appearance of substantial numbers of them in minor political leadership rôles. Along with it would come, of course, a great deal of tension as such groups increased in power and numbers, and the first phase would probably not be attractive in its quality and style. We might expect, moreover, that the very same liberal, socially conscious groups now urging a "fair shake" for our minorities may themselves soon be embarking on new reform crusades without quite realizing what was happening. It has all happened in the past.

But what *would* be happening? It would be the same process of assimilation and socialization, the same "mobility-cycle" (though they did not call it that) which was undergone by the Irish after the Civil War, and after them the Jews and Italians. It is a process full of corruption and full of vitality. What we know about *those* groups may well give us the clues we need for plotting what is still to come.

*Monte A. Calvert*

# THE MANIFEST FUNCTIONS OF THE MACHINE

*How well did the political boss, in comparison with the professional urban specialist, administer his city? Investigating the manifest functions of the machine rather than its latent ones, Monte Calvert finds that the boss was a good technical administrator who often displayed a broad developmental view of urban growth. He was the unspecialized professional who realized that large sums of money had to be spent for urban expansion and improve-*

Reprinted by permission of the author. Excerpted from a paper, "Technical Decision-Making in a Political Context: The American City, 1850–1925," presented to the conference on Social Science Concepts in American Political History held at the State University College at Brockport, New York, October 25, 1969.

*ment. If this is so, might the boss serve as a model for the type of leadership our cities need today? Monte Calvert has studied one aspect of the engineering profession in his work* The Mechanical Engineer in America, 1830–1910.

Since the sociologist Robert Merton in the late 1950's pointed out (or reminded us of) the latent functions of the political machine (mobility access, welfare, etc.), avant-garde historians have been concerned with the extra-curricular activities of bosses and the failure of reformers to grasp that what immigrants and other city people needed was help, not moralism. Some of us have even been accused of venturing into a sort of Neo-Romanticism concerning the political boss, a romanticism strengthened by the sad and troublous times which now have befallen our cities, even though they are presumably run by the progressive credos of honesty, civil service, and efficiency. Such concern with the beneficient character, however haphazard, of the latent functions of the machine has tended to take attention away from the just as important manifest functions of the machine, such as the economical and efficient running of a big, complex city.

I might also suggest that down deep in most of us is a wellspring of progressive moralism. No matter how much we are able to rationalize the benefits of boss rule, it is nonetheless corrupt and thus immoral. We find it hard to resist implicit normative emotional judgments, even though we can be rational intellectually. . . .

To represent the urban boss as a stander against professionalism ignores the fact that his emergence is also the beginning of professional control and administration of American cities. American cities began to lose their sense of community in the 1840's with spectacular growth and, in many cases, large Irish immigration. This produced a crisis in the administration of urban services which was exacerbated by a not entirely explainable sudden rise in the level of expectations of the urban population. The result was a very new kind of urban polity emerging in the 1850's.

That decade produced the first major attempt by many American cities to establish their independence from state legislatures, to become responsible for new types of urban services, and to consolidate the municipal corporation. One of the vital changes, related to the loss of community and to sheer growth, was the elimination of voluntarism in supplying urban services. As long as a city felt itself one community or even a set of communities, it was possible for volunteer fire companies to function. By the 1850's these volunteer companies were beginning to be phased out, sometimes completely replaced by city-paid and run professional fire departments. Street paving was handled traditionally by requiring three days' labor or the equivalent in money from each male citizen. Abuse of the system, the difficulty of getting immigrant groups to cooperate, and again sheer growth in size and amount of traffic caused many cities in the 1850's to establish departments of streets which were given general tax monies to hire private contractors to do street repair work. The same thing occurred with sewers, sidewalks, and curbs. Besides a vast increase in the amount of such work being done in the 1850's (street paving, sewer building, etc., often increased 1000 to 5000 per cent in this decade, greater than any other decade in most cities except the late 1880's and early 1890's), this change had another striking result. Whereas city government had been relatively informal before 1850—prominent businessmen, doctors, lawyers, and editors often served on city councils without pay and sat infrequently—after 1850 the very lucrative contracts for paving streets and laying sewers led to the emergence of professional city politicians, whose services were required on a full-time basis.

Coupled with the emergence of this new power group was the fact that the public works themselves required vast amounts of unskilled labor which was supplied by the newly arrived, unemployed immigrants. Here we have the genesis of the urban machine, with close cooperation between city bosses, major contractors, and immigrants, who were both workers and voters. This was the system that old-stock, upper-middle-class reformers were to fight intermittently, without too much success, from the 1860's to the 1930's and even beyond in some cities.

Most urban services not supplied by voluntary community action before 1850 were supplied by private companies. These services included water supply, gas lighting, rubbish removal, street cleaning, and mass transit, and each company needed a franchise to operate, allowing it to supply a particular service to a part or all of a city, excluding any other companies. These franchises had often proved unprofitable, particularly in the case of water supply in which the companies found themselves unable to keep up with growing demand for service without continually going into debt for new pumping stations, reservoirs, and pipelines. This was partly due to a general feeling on the part of many that water should be free, that it was like air and sunshine, the property of all. This does not seem to have been true of gas lighting and street railway franchises, although they probably were not very profitable before the 1850's or later. As a result, by the 1850's many of these services had become recognized as natural monopolies, and there was considerable agitation for municipalities to buy all such facilities and operate them for the public benefit. In a few cases municipal ownership did occur, but it seems that just about the time it was being discussed, some of the franchises began to pay off. [The 1850's then can be seen as the era when supplying urban services became big business and profitable business for the first time and provided the potential patronage for sustaining a political machine, which engendered the first political professionals.]

A prime example is Boss W. M. Tweed of New York. In his early period he began centralizing the previously disorganized enterprises of city officials, particularly raising the scale of operations. Under Tweed all city street cleaning was done by one organization. Twice the city's governmental structure was overhauled in the interest of efficiency. It is not clear that all this could have been accomplished in any other way, even though the second efficiency reorganization cost Tweed $600,000 in graft to get through the New York legislature. [I would like to suggest here that there are acceptable levels of graft within any culture and that within WASP American culture the permissible level tolerated stands at about 10 to 15 per cent. When the graft level rose above this figure, a reform movement was bound to appear.] By the late 1860's the graft level in general had risen from 10 to 15 per cent to 30 per cent, which was not acceptable to the business leadership that had supported Tweed, and he was thrown out of power in the early 1870's. However, the business community did support him in his drive for growth rather than consolidation.

\* \* \*

. . . [The issue of growth versus consolidation] . . . appears frequently in this period. [An] example is the paving of Washington, D.C., forever different from other American cities because of its function and the nature of its population. In 1870 the city had not yet taken its present monumental form and was a swampy mudhole covered with flimsy wooden buildings. Pennsylvania Avenue was so hilly and uneven that it was not possible to see the White House from the Capitol and vice versa as originally planned. The city was such a physical mess of unpaved and ungraded streets, open sewers, and disorganized building that there was serious talk of moving the capital to some place in the Midwest and abandoning the city entirely. Two events in the 1870's changed this drift and assured that the capital would stay in Washington: Congress authorized the construction of a new million-dollar-plus building to house the War, Navy, and State departments, and Alexander Shepherd became boss of the public works department of the city. In 1871 the District was given a territorial style government with commissioners. Shepherd, a native Washingtonian of good social and financial standing, cared about his city and felt that only a comprehensive effort to pave and grade the streets, install sewers, and street lights would keep the capital permanently there. But the transient and part-time nature of the city's population meant that many people whose permanent homes were elsewhere did not wish to pay taxes to improve two cities. The large taxpayers advocated a slow, pay-as-you-go plan for public improvements, but Shepherd felt that unless substantial gains were made at once the city would not progress fast enough to keep up with other American cities. It might be noted that Shepherd was also a highly successful speculator in residential real estate development and had strong personal reasons for wanting public improvements. Using tactics any Tammany leader would have been proud of, Shepherd railroaded through a massive public improvement bill which called for millions of dollars of expenditures in several years.

Rather than starting from the center of the street and building continuous streets outward, Shepherd at once began paving streets and parts of streets all over the city, and the paved sections did not connect. He increased the number of salaried employees in the street department from 10 to 203. Even though a bond issue, opposed by conservative Washingtonians, passed by 12 to 1, Shep-

herd's enemies had launched a Congressional investigation by
1872. But by the spring of 1873 the physical changes already be-
coming apparent in the city took the wind out of his critics sails;
the frenzied activity had given new life to the city. And because he
had begun paving operations all over the city at once, Shepherd
had widespread support. The panic of 1873 forced financial strin-
gency and caused, by 1874, another investigation. Also, Shepherd
had unfortunately chosen to pave many streets with a then experi-
mental wood-block paving, which was undeniably quieter than
stone, but which by 1874 had already begun to rot. In three years
the district had run up a debt larger than that of all but seven
states. Shepherd was finally ousted, lost his fortune, and retired in
1876 with his family to Mexico. But, however fiscally irresponsible
he may have been, Shepherd had gotten things moving . . . .
Much of the work was turned over to the Army Corps of Engineers,
and by 1890 the paving of Washington was complete, making it,
along with Denver, Colorado, one of the two best paved cities in
the country. Whatever one might say about Boss Shepherd, his
actions brought Washington all the way from the bottom to the top
in terms of urban improvements, and in less than twenty years.

Boss Shepherd has traditionally been accused of failing to consult experts in his decision to use wood block as a paving material
as it soon rotted. But at that time, if he had consulted experts, he
would have found wood blocks in high favor, and its use continued
for over a generation in special applications, such as for quiet
areas around hospitals and schools. It was used in some cities,
such as Milwaukee, until about 1900. Critics also opposed Shepherd's plan for filling in the Washington Canal and building a sewer
system; his critics suggested using Washington Canal as an open
sewer. Engineering opinion in this case would have upheld Shepherd. Obviously one cannot conclude that machine politicians utilized poor engineering judgment, nor that reformers, concerned
with lowering costs before 1895, used good engineering judgment.
The city of Newark, for example, in 1879 received a sober engineering report that suggested they use the abandoned Morris Canal as
a water supply system and the socialists who came to power in
Milwaukee in 1910 made bad engineering judgments on paving
materials which resulted in a lowering of standards.

[The actual success of the bosses limited the growth of professionalism among urban engineers, but there were other factors
too.] Between 1870 and 1890 many cities sought to compare their
problems and to reach relatively scientific conclusions, but each
city faced quite different problems. One of the earliest of national
urban reforms, for example, was the agitation for improved urban
housing standards, particularly for the poor and working classes.
The conditions in each major city were, however, quite different.
In New York rapid growth and space limitations resulted in the
development of the high-rise multi-family tenement house, and
working class housing was a serious problem. In Boston, however,
less stringent space conditions and a much slower growth rate resulted in the wood-framed triple-decker suburban house, whereas
Philadelphia, with rather unlimited space for expansion, developed
in a unique fashion, resembled only by Baltimore and a few other
smaller cities. In Philadelphia the three-bedroom, single-family brick
row house was most common, and very early an inside kitchen, a
complete bathroom, and a window in every room were standard
features of every dwelling. Here, at least in the 1870–1910 period,
when these dwellings were relatively new, there was no urban poor
housing problem. The problems and the answers of one city did
not fit another. The growth of professionalism was limited by this lack
of a uniform body of knowledge. [It is interesting to note, in the case
of housing codes, for example, that most improvements had become
well nigh universal before codes were adopted. The facts preceded
the codes, and the codes were often a validation of existing standards, set up by public expectations.] . . .

[Another factor limiting urban engineering professionalism was
the attitude of the pre-1895 reformers regarding expenditures and
taxes. They believed in a mythology of lower taxes, despite increased demand for services.] Ironically, in the few cases when
they achieved power, they found themselvs in the position of cur-
tailing services and raising taxes; they continued to be surprised
when they were turned out of office at the next election by the local
machine, using the slogan "look at your tax bill." This suggests two
things: that reformers were not as efficient as the bosses or that
they did not have the access to information and expertise as the
bosses. Also, it would tend to work against any connection be-

tween this type of reformer and the professional city engineer. Any professional wants to have money to spend.

Up to now we have been looking at the bosses and their critics, the early urban reformers, but have said little about engineers. Was there a rising class of professional engineers concerned with urban engineering problems? Yes and no.

First it is important to note that the availability of cosmopolitan experts depended very much on the time and which urban service one considers; engineering itself was in the process of professionalizing. Water supply was a problem that almost from the first required expert opinion, though this was often contradictory. In sewerage Ellis Chesborough in the 1850's began a role as a cosmopolitan sewerage and drainage engineer, and many more were to follow. Street paving, by contrast, remained until very late (the early twentieth century) a local, empirical, nonprofessional activity. Street lighting, because it was a national entrepreneurial enterprise in many respects, developed national standards, less under pressure from reform governments than from within the industry itself. Here the United Gas Improvement Company was the operating factor since it controlled the basic patents in the gas field. It just happened to be progressive and run largely by engineers. The development of the concept of a professional city engineer with responsibilities in all these areas is clearly a development of the 1890's and the early twentieth century.

The mid-nineties also mark, I would suggest, deep changes in the type of urban reformers appearing. Reform was no longer a taxpayer's revolt but was supported by the business elites and rising professionals who previously had given at least tacit assent to the dynamic activities of the urban bosses.

The professional city engineer was introduced by the new progressive type of urban reformer who wanted expertise, professionalism, efficiency, and bureaucratic methods. He comes hand in hand with the growth of bureaus of municipal research, both public and private, which provided information of a technical and financial nature. Certainly the political machines were essentially entrepreneurial—this was a source of their strength—as they could be ruthless in the process of reorganization and did not have the dysfunctions and inefficiencies of bureaucracy to reckon with. Yet the progressives liked to believe they were both scientific and tough-minded. The idea of a technocratic rule of the American city was not foreign to their conceptions, and it bore fruit as the city manager movement, of which more later. However, the continued naïveté and apparent lack of access to information displayed by the reformers in power continued to sabotage their efforts. Trying to imitate the organizational skills of the machine, they merely succeeded in transforming entrepreneurial success into bureaucratic morass. One case in point is the term of Morris L. Cooke, protégé of scientific management experts and director of public works in Philadelphia in the reform Blankenburg administration in 1911. Cooke constantly found himself confronted with dilemmas regarding ideology and practice. Although he believed that there should be open competition for Philadelphia's garbage contract on a yearly basis, it took him some time to realize that there was likely to be only one firm in the running, the one connected with the previous machine. No other firm was going to build an expensive garbage reduction plant on the hope that it might get the contract at best every other year.

\*        \*        \*

[A] factor which might be related to professionalism and modernism in general is the centralization and uniform administration of urban services. However, there is no clear connection between centralization of services and decentralization as reform objectives. It seems that the reformers were reasonably pragmatic about their approach to this problem and sought whichever would lower costs directly. One suggested hypothesis is that in the largest cities decentralization of services may have provided the desired results for the reform group; in smaller cities where there was a single power elite, composed of the business leadership, centralization may have been the key. Another factor was the extent to which the cities were homogeneous economically, politically, and ethnically. In some cities the movement toward centralized control by a city-wide department of public works seems related to more generalized, progressive attitudes toward efficiency engineering, centralized planning by trained experts, and elimination of graft in public works contracts. In other cities, most notably New York, the situation seems somewhat reversed: centralization of services was connected with wide-scale improvement at general public expense and was organized by the machine, particularly by Boss Tweed. Whether centralization was the issue of the bosses or the reformers may not be so important as the more down to earth practical devices. One device that was consistently used by the middle and upper class reformers was to push for shifting the burden of street improvement to the taxpayers who owned the abutting property. This meant less cost to the well-to-do taxpayers, since they were not paying for improvements in slum or immigrant areas. These areas often would not be paved or improved under such a system; often the land was owned by well-off slumlords who did not choose to improve the neighborhood. The percentage of improvement costs paid by the community and the percentage paid by the owner of the abutting land is a significant variable. It changes over time in most cities and it varies at any time from 0 per cent to 10 per cent paid by the municipality.

In conclusion, I would like to suggest several concepts and themes which are implicit in what I have said.

1. Few urban technical decisions are without political, economic, or social contexts.
2. Neither the bosses nor the reformers had any corner on the best technical advice. If anything, the bosses had a broader developmental viewpoint.
3. It is possible to see the boss as manifestly a good technical administrator as well as a friendly Irishman with sticky fingers.
4. Our values tell us that boss rule was inherently inefficient, but we know that ward leaders and other machine officials worked incredibly long hours, were to some extent working for themselves, and were in constant danger of being dumped if they were not efficient.
5. We can easily rationalize graft up to the 10–15 per cent level as simply the money necessary for party expenses, which in any case would have to come from some source.
6. It may be that illicit networks and organizations are more efficient than licit ones (see the comments of Daniel Bell in *The End of Ideology,* pp. 115–36, 381–82).
7. Certainly the technical decisions made by the bosses in the late nineteenth century seem adaptive, inexpensive, and basi-

cally much sounder than the decisions we are now making in centralized, bureaucratically controlled cities with civil service systems and professionalism (at least in city planning) running rampant.

8. I would suggest a reevaluation of the claims of specialized professionalism and a seeking for models for the unspecialized professional. The urban boss may provide that model.

9. I would also like to posit a basic conflict in the American urban polity between two mentalities, a real estate mentality and a taxpayer mentality. The real estate mentality, belongs to developers, speculators, and business interests desiring expansion and growth, and the taxpayer mentality characterizes home owners, nonexpansive "lumpen bourgeoisie" business interests.

Here was, of course, the prime function of the boss. He convinced business leaders that to have urban growth, expansion, and improvement, money—large sums of it—must be spent. In a sense the boss set the stage for progressive-type professionalism: the bosses' habit of getting things done became at least an unconscious, but more likely a conscious attitude among the progressives. The progressives and the bosses had much in common, something we cannot say of the pre-1895 reformers, but there was of course always a basic difference, one which we have not yet resolved. The bosses dictum was "give people what they want," rather than the progressives "give people what we think they should have."

*Seymour Mandelbaum*

# BOSS TWEED'S NEW YORK

*In his study of* Boss Tweed's New York, *Seymour Mandelbaum finds that city to have been severely fragmented, only loosely held together by its means of transportation and communications. It was the role of the political*

Reprinted by permission from Seymour Mandelbaum, *Boss Tweed's New York* (New York, 1965), pp. 66–75, 182. Copyright © 1965 by John Wiley & Sons, Inc., Publishers.

*boss to bind together this fragmented society. The boss's simple answer to complex problems was often the big payoff. Thus the boss, like most of society during the days of Tweed, relied upon the free operations of the marketplace to run the social machinery.*

The victory of the Democrats in the state election of 1869 linked Albany to City Hall. The "moment of opportunity," became Tweed's moment. The drive towards improvement was captured, broadened, and finally damned. The history of Tweed's rise and fall, Kelly's ascendency and limitation, is a measure of the collapse of a broad-scale attack on the "problem" of the city. New York, divided and tamed overly-ambitious public entrepreneurs.

William Marcy Tweed, for all his bulk, is a man hidden in the shadows of Thomas Nast's leering cartoons in *Harpers Weekly.* The other members of his ring were real enough. A. Oakey Hall, Mayor from 1869 to 1872, covered a keen and, one suspects, brooding intelligence with an exterior mask at once a little too witty and a little too elegant. Peter Sweeny, Tweed's adviser and parks commissioner, was a well-trained lawyer of skill and sophistication. Under attack, he remained scornfully aggressive and contemptuous of his detractors. Richard Connolly, city comptroller, was an obsequious man. Fearful of being victimized by his friends, in the last days of the Tweed Ring he turned to his enemies for support and justification. Used and then spurned, he ended as a pitiful, if wealthy, object of contempt.

The Boss himself is more difficult to characterize. In Nast's portraits, Tweed is a lecherous, corrupt, and powerful Falstaff. Bargaining for pardon in the later seventies, he displayed a softness which fit this image. Sweeny, he complained, was a "hard, overbearing, revengeful man." What is missing from the image is an explanation of Tweed's real personal powers, his ability to ingratiate himself with men of respectability and with low politicians, his breadth of political imagination and his vindictiveness. All one can say about Tweed is that he was predictable. He united the elements in a divided society in the only manner in which they could be united: by paying them off. Attracted to a scorned profession, he acted with scorn for conventional social ethics. Like so many American entrepreneurs, he maximized his short run profits and then got out.

Tweed's climb to political power was a classic American success story. Even his setbacks stood him in good stead. He rose through the ranks rapidly as leader of a local volunteer fire company, alderman, and then congressman. Two years in Washington bored him, but in 1854 he had the political good fortune to be defeated for reelection by a candidate of the nativist (Know-Nothing) American party. The badge of his defeat was helpful in a city soon to have a large Catholic voting population. After the election he accepted a post as commissioner in the Board of Education where his hand touched building and supply contracts. He was elected to the new Board of Supervisors of the County of New York in 1857. The board flourished on the profits realized from the painfully slow and costly construction of a new County Court House.

The Democratic party in New York was severely divided from 1857 to 1865 by controversy growing out of the Civil War crisis. Democratic dissension allowed the election of a Republican mayor in 1861 and the victory of the candidate of a splinter Democratic faction two years later. At the end of the war unity was restored. Tammany Hall, led by Tweed and Sweeny, emerged as the dominant political organization in the city, hardly challenged by the remnants of rival groups and working closely with the national party leaders in New York. Tammany's candidate, John T. Hoffman, was elected mayor in 1866. The Democratic National Convention of 1868, which nominated former Governor Horatio Seymour to oppose Grant for the presidency, was held in Tammany's resplendent new building, finished just in time to accommodate the delegates. In the fall, Tweed gave the voters a considerable hand in carrying New York for Seymour. Hoffman was elected governor and was replaced by Hall in the mayor's office. The Democracy captured the state legislature for the first time in twenty years in the election of 1869.

Tweed was a master of the strategy of the leadership which succeeds because it allows men to do as they please. The Board of Education allowed teachers in predominately Catholic neighborhoods to put aside the little Protestant rituals of the American public school. The police and excise boards smiled on both the men who filled the cups and the imbibers. The Sabbath could be enjoyed in

New York with drink in hand despite a state law which prohibited the sale of liquor on Sunday.

Tweed was a master communicator. With massive sums of money at his disposal, he united the fragmented news media. Several reporters on each paper received stipends from city officials to ensure favorable coverage. Public advertising supported both the largest newspapers and the host of tiny journals smiling favorably at the Boss. "Bought" stories in out-of-town papers were reprinted in New York and "created the impression that the entire nation admired the city government."

More positively, and with a fresher hand, Tweed rallied diverse groups behind his programs. He encouraged Catholic allegiance to the Democracy by a policy of state and city aid to parochial schools and private charities. The Church received nearly $1,500,000 from public sources between 1869 and 1871. Labor unions were encouraged to organize and allowed to strike. Tweed energetically promoted the development program and the reorganization of the city government. His policies won support in high and respectable circles. His implicit motto was "something for everyone." His tactical plan was "do it now." Andrew Green and the Central Park Commission argued for restrained growth and a careful regard for costs; Tweed and his associates, for unlimited expansion and far-ranging public expenditures.

\*       \*       \*

Democrats had long protested the absence of home rule. The need for governmental coordination of expanding activities allied them with groups of normally hostile businessmen anxious to bring order and efficiency out of chaos. Mayor Hall in his annual message in January, 1870 pointed out the anomalies of city government. Three different sets of officials controlled the streets. Each of the major departments presented an independent budget to the legislature and controlled its own expenditures. The metropolitan police were legally independent of local ordinances and supervision. The mayor was a figurehead unable to control his subordinates.

The passage of a new charter in 1870, which Tweed admitted cost him at least $600,000, did not entirely cut through this tangle but it did promise to simplify city government and to centralize responsibility. The commissions were abolished and city departments were established in their place. The mayor's control remained marginal but he was allowed at least to appoint the department heads. The major beneficiary of the concentration of authority was Tweed, as superintendent of public works. The greater part of the city development projects, including responsibility for uptown streets, which had previously belonged to the Central Park Commission, was placed in his hands. The superintendent was appointed for a term of four years and could be removed from office only after a trial before the Court of Common Pleas.

The charter promised financial order where there was only chaos. A special Board of Audit was created to close the affairs of the redundant county offices. The board was authorized to audit the liabilities of the county and to issue, in payment, revenue bonds redeemable from the tax levy of 1871. A consolidated bond was also approved. Municipal finances were still largely directed at Albany, but the city gained greater control over its own taxes and debt than it had ever enjoyed before. Samuel Jones Tilden, chairman of the New York State Democratic Committee, denounced the proposed charter as a scheme of despotic government foreign to the American system. The old philanthropist Peter Cooper, for the Citizen's Association, on the other hand, lauded the charter as it was being debated in the legislature. After its passage, the membership of the association endorsed the document. The endorsement was signed by a long list of prominent New Yorkers led by James Brown, the venerable head of the most esteemed private banking firm in the city, and John Jacob Astor, probably the largest private owner of real estate in New York.

At every step, Tweed associated his ambitious political program with his own personal interests. He indulged in a pattern of multiple office holding which would have warmed the heart of an eighteenth century placeman. He was at one and the same time superintendent of public works, county supervisor, state senator, Grand Sachem of the Tammany Society, chairman of the Democratic-Republican General Committee of the City of New York (Tammany Hall), and supervisor of the County Court House. Together with his friends and relatives, he speculated extensively in city real estate.

The city Boss joined hands with the arch speculators and

business titans of his day. Jay Gould engaged Tweed's aid during the great battle with Cornelius Vanderbilt of the New York Central for control of the Erie Railroad in 1868. The Boss used his influence with New York judges and secured the passage of a law altering the method of electing Erie's board of directors in Gould's favor. Judge Albert Cardoza, one of Tweed's faithful legion, protected Gould in 1869 from paying his debts after an unsuccessful attempt to corner the gold market. The Erie received special privileges in the transportation of westward-bound immigrants from the reception center at Castle Garden. Tweed, in return, was elected to the Erie board and received Gould's political aid in the counties along the railroad's route.

Tweed was not sparing with his gifts. With the titans at peace, he served as Vanderbilt's legislative representative in Albany. The owners of land on the East Side pressed the city in 1871 to force Vanderbilt's New York and Harlem River Railroad to cover its tracks along Fourth Avenue. The Commodore, with Tweed's support, consented only to sink the tracks below the street level and successfully demanded that the city pay half the cost of improvement.

The Central Park Commission, reorganized as a Parks Department, was an important prize in Tweed's battle to control the city. The park system became a tool for political manipulation. Green remained on the board but was stripped of his executive powers. These were shared by Sweeny as president and by Henry Hilton as vice-president and treasurer. Hilton was the legal counsel and business associate of A. T. Stewart, the largest dry-goods merchant in the city. Old employees were dismissed and the work force was enlarged, probably, as Green contended, to provide for political favorites. The board established handsome administrative quarters for itself.

At the same time that they exploited the patronage of the Parks Department, the new commissioners attempted serious changes in policy. They granted private amusement and refreshment concessions in Central Park. Several alterations were made in the basic plan of the park, designed to facilitate movement and to provide for more formal recreational areas. The changes in and of themselves, Frederick Law Olmsted, the park's original designer, later admitted, were not necessarily deleterious but they violated his unified conception of structure and landscape and intruded upon his attempt to relieve dreary "urban conditions" by providing open and natural vistas. The changes projected the city into the park.

In addition to changing the design of Central Park, the new commissioners shifted funds from the giant park to speed improvement of small parks and squares downtown. This shift represented a change in the distribution of benefits between social groups and also reflected a respect for the possibility of distinctly urban forms of excitement and recreation. Olmsted, assuming that the urban environment was inevitably dreary, attempted to relieve the monotony by a greenbelt of parks which would bring the country into the city. He envisioned his parks as community centers which would bring "closely together, poor and rich, young and old, Jew and Gentile" in a "social, neighborly, unexertive form of recreation." He insisted that the parks should present a sharp contrast to the "restraining and confining conditions of the town . . . which compel us to walk circumspectly, watchfully, jealously, . . . to look closely upon others without sympathy."

Olmsted's imagination leaped to a vision of the city as a united community. Practically, since movement was difficult and costly, his park for all became a park for the better half of society. The Parks Department, with a narrower and more fragmented image, focused on smaller urban neighborhood centers. Sweeny could not afford to share Olmsted's scorn for the "young men in knots of perhaps half a dozen in lounging attitudes rudely obstructing the sidewalks" or descending into a "brilliantly lighted basement, where they find others of their sort, see, hear, smell, drink, and eat all manner of vile things." The public square extended the sidewalk and basement rather than refuting them.

Finally, Tweed made the public treasury his own. Just as he paid others, he charged the city handsomely for his services. Every city contractor padded his bills to finance a "rake-off" for the Boss and his friends. In this thievery, Tweed was undone, the "moment of opportunity" spent, and the costs of urban coordination through a giant "pay-off" revealed.

\* \* \*

Within New York, the narrow lines of communication between

men and their limited ability to deal with complex information fragmented society. The men who made important decisions were forced to simplify complex problems. Decentralized decision-making was embedded in both the values and the practice of the city. The most common form of decentralization—and simplification— was reliance upon the free operations of the market place. Tweed's purchases of political support and his thievery were simply the ultimate extension of the dominance of the dollar-vote. Centralization or coordination intended to limit reliance upon the market loomed in the minds of New York's isolated citizens as illegitimate autocracy.

*Joel A. Tarr*
# THE URBAN POLITICIAN AS ENTREPRENEUR

*In the following selection, Joel A. Tarr discusses why so many machine politicians regarded politics as a business. The social backgrounds and self-made character of these politicians may explain why American urban politics has been traditionally more involved with tangibles, such as patronage jobs, than with ideology. For the machine politician, the use of politics for private gain simply followed George Washington Plunkitt's assertion that "when a man works in politics, he should get something out of it." Professor Tarr has also written* A Study in Boss Politics: William Lorimer of Chicago.

In the late nineteenth and early twentieth centuries America's expanding urban areas beckoned like magnets to those in search of their fortunes. Millions of European immigrants as well as native farm migrants took jobs in the city's factories, its mercantile marts or loaded a peddler's pushcart, embracing the basic entrepreneurial thrust of American society. But for some new urbanites, politics rather than the factory or pushcart was the avenue chosen to seek

Reprinted by permission of the author. This is a revised version of Joel A. Tarr, "The Urban Politician as Entrepreneur," *Mid-America,* 49 (January 1967), pp. 55–67.

economic reward. This applied particularly to the urban political boss and members of his political machine; their entry into politics was primarily motivated by an expectation of material reward rather than the desire to achieve governmental or ideological ends.

The typical urban boss was a man who regarded politics as a business and who used his power for personal and party gain. He was a businessman whose chief stock in trade was the goods of the political world—influence, laws, government grants, and franchises —which he utilized to make a private profit. In short, he was a "political entrepreneur." In the words of boss Richard Croker of Tammany Hall, "Like a business man in business, I work for my own pocket all the time." And he used, as political scientists Edward Banfield and James Q. Wilson note, "inducements that . . . [were] both *specific* and *material*" to hold his machine together. In the 1880's, Lord Bryce observed the same phenomena: "the desire for office, and for office as a means of *gain*" cements the machine.

One explanation for the tendency of the boss or machine politician to regard politics as a business was their social origins. Most urban machine politicians and bosses had risen from humble and immigrant backgrounds; usually their religious orientation was Roman Catholic or some other nonpietistic type of belief. Professor Harold Zink's study of twenty municipal bosses reveals that fifteen were raised in the city slums; fifteen also were either immigrants or the children of immigrants. A number were forced into the streets at a young age to help support their families. Studies of Chicago and New York machine politicians in the late nineteenth and early twentieth centuries show the same type of lower-class background and foreign origins for the great majority of those examined.

The machine politician's background helps explain his attitude towards and motivation in politics. His humble and immigrant origins, as well as his nonpietistic religious beliefs, caused him to look upon politics as a vehicle for advancement rather than as a means to reform the social order. He lacked what Richard Hofstadter calls the "Yankee-Protestant" conception of politics—a conception that involved using the state as an instrument to reform the morals of the populace and that idealized public service as a duty to be undertaken for the "good" of the community. The machine politician expected a reward for his services. George Washington Plunkitt of

Tammany Hall once said that although he might differ with other politicians on "tariffs and currencies and all them things," they agreed on "the main proposition that when a man works in politics, he should get something out of it." The deprived economic background of most machine politicians required that they secure a return for their efforts. The wealthy businessman or elite reformer in politics was freed of this necessity.

Politics also furnished a ladder of mobility for the immigrant at a time when other doors to success were closed to him. In politics a particular ethnic background was often an asset, as support came from national loyalty. The bosses carefully balanced slates of candidates with members of the city's leading nationality groups. Any number of urban politicans rose to positions of status and power as their particular ethnic groups came to dominate the city. In Chicago, for instance, Irishmen and Germans, as well as native Americans, were most prominent in the city's politics during the late nineteenth century; after 1900, however, as the "New Immigrants" flooded into the city, increasing numbers of Bohemians, Poles, and Russian Jews appeared. Politics thus provided an alternative form of social and economic mobility to those who found other channels blocked because of a lack of native family roots, wealth, or education.

The self-made character of the bosses, and their antagonism to "reformers," generally made them advocates of the status quo. They, as well as many of their immigrant constituents, looked upon reform as a sham. There was "No Place for Reformers Among Bohemians," editorialized the Chicago Bohemian newspaper *Denni Hlasatel:* "We have with us many reformers, but their work does not meet with much success. The reason for this is that people do not take much stock in the sincerity of their uplifting exhortations. . . . They conduct this agitation to satisfy their own political ambitions. . . ." Political machines often acted as social welfare organizations, but they never posed a threat to the structure of their society. In the 1896 election, Democratic bosses in New York and Chicago favored the conservative Gold Democrat ticket rather than the more radical Bryan. During the progressive period, many bosses fought the direct democracy proposals of the progressives and efforts at social and economic legislation because they perceived such measures as a threat to their control.

Just as their business allies found opportunities for gain in the needs of the growing cities of the late nineteenth century, so did the political boss. Especially common was what Plunkitt of Tammany called "honest graft": involvement in businesses that would benefit from the boss's political influence. Another frequent practice was that of "boodling," where the politician sold his vote on matters such as franchises to the businessman. Oftentimes businessmen would be forced to pay as much to prevent legislation as to obtain it. Public funds were frequently deposited in banks that made "loans" to politicians or in which politicians held stock. Tax assessments were raised or lowered depending upon the generosity of the person or corporation being taxed. And, politicians often pocketed large sums secured through the holding of fee offices or the retaining of bank interest upon public deposits.

An examination of the political situation in one city, Chicago, will help demonstrate the great extent to which the machine politician and the boss engaged in political entrepreneurship. Chicago was, to use Nelson Algren's term, a "city on the make." Its motto was "I will," and growing population and industry demonstrated its vitality. During the years from 1871–1893, the land area of the "Windy City" increased more than fivefold, while its population spurted from 300,000 to over a million. Much of this increase was due to European immigrants. By 1890 77.9 percent of the city's population was of foreign parentage, mainly German, Irish, English, and Scandinavian; during the decade of the 90's, increasing numbers of eastern and southern Europeans swelled the city's size.

The swift growth of Chicago with its immigrant population created an ideal situation for the emergence of a system of political machines and bosses. In the process of expanding its borders, Chicago incorporated a number of governmental jurisdictions, many of which maintained their separate functions. This condition, along with the confusion created by over-lapping city, county, and state jurisdictions, produced a fragmentation of power. A businessman who desired something from the city would often have to deal with multiple agencies, any of which might block his request or demand payment for passing it on to the next.

The political machines that arose in both major parties altered this situation by centralizing political power. The businessman who wanted a municipal contract or license could go directly to the boss, eliminating duplication and confusion, and usually paying a cheaper price than if he had used the regular channels. In return for his services, the boss would be paid a sum or receive a contribution to the party chest. This, in turn, further tightened his hold over the machine by giving him control of campaign funds.

The political organizations themselves rested on the new urban migrants, usually European immigrants. Basically unfamiliar with American political institutions and democratic ideals, the immigrant was bewildered about what to do with his vote. The political machine gave him the answer: they treated the vote as a form of currency. They paid him for it or, in return for following the precinct worker's instructions at election time, the immigrant received various welfare services: a turkey at Christmas, a bucket of coal in the cold of winter, or a job in the city public works department. In the Chicago immigrant wards the machines had a practically guaranteed base of votes coming from immigrants who were indebted for favors.

Controlling each of the machines were political bosses. The key figures in the Democratic party organization were Roger C. Sullivan and John P. Hopkins. Heading the Republican was Congressman and later Senator William Lorimer, the "Blond Boss." Sullivan and Hopkins although born in this country were of Irish descent; Lorimer was born in Manchester, England, of Scottish parents and came to the United States when he was four years old. Sullivan's father, a farmer, and Lorimer's father, an itinerant Presbyterian minister, both died when the future politicians were young boys, forcing them into the streets to help support their families. As a result, neither had more than a few years of formal education. Hopkins was more fortunate, earning a degree at St. Joseph's College in Buffalo, New York. Sullivan and Hopkins each held elected office only once: Hopkins was Mayor of Chicago in 1894–95, while Sullivan was Cook County Probate Court Clerk in 1890–94. Both, however, occupied numerous official party posts. Lorimer was a more consistent candidate for public office, serving as Congress-man for the terms 1894–1900 and 1902–1909, and as Senator for 1909–1912.

These men exercised their influence mainly through the county and state political committees and at nominating conventions. Lorimer was chairman of the Republican Cook County Central Committee for most of the period 1895–1904; Hopkins was chairman of the Democratic State Central Committee 1901–04; and Sullivan was Illinois National Committeeman 1904–16. Lorimer headed a traditional hierarchical party organization with its base on Chicago's West Side; his alliances extended throughout the county and state. Sullivan and Hopkins had a more casual organization with influence in scattered Chicago wards, but also particularly on the West Side and in the "River Wards" where the immigrant vote was concen-trated.

In addition to the "big bosses" there were other important com-ponents of the Chicago political world. The city was divided into thirty-five wards and each ward was represented on the City Council by two aldermen. Each ward also had a representative on the Republican and on the Democratic Cook County Central Committees and Chicago Central Committees; the county committees were the real political ruling bodies. The city was divided into state senatorial districts as well as wards, and these districts elected one senator and three representatives to the Illinois General Assembly. Because cumulative proportional voting was used in General Assem-bly elections, there were no real election contests. The machines divided the three seats among themselves and then nominated only three candidates. The result was that each machine controlled blocs of representatives in the state legislature. The dominant power in each ward might hold no elected post or might serve in the City Council, the General Assembly, or even in Congress, but almost always he held a seat on the county committee. Although some ward leaders ruled as feudal lords, paying homage to no leader, most served in one machine or the other.

As far as can be determined politicians on every level of the machine above the precinct level engaged in political entrepreneur-ship, using their political influence as a wedge to secure economic gain. The extent of profit and involvement depended upon the politician's power and influence. Perhaps most common was vote selling, a practice followed by many aldermen (the "gray wolves") and by assemblymen. Among those who bought, for instance, was traction magnate Charles Tyson Yerkes who wanted franchises for his streetcar interests, the Chicago "Gas Trust," or perhaps, as occurred in the 1909 General Assembly, a furniture company anxious to secure a state contract. In the 1909 Assembly, and probably in others, there was a jackpot distributed among the legislators; it was the creation of corporations interested in preventing or obtaining certain legislation.

On another level one could find many examples of "honest graft." Coal and bonding companies were popular among the politicians; all government buildings needed coal; courts and many public officials required bondsmen. Lorimer was a silent partner in the O'Gara King Coal Company which had large contracts with the city, county, and state governments. Other Chicago politicans who owned coal companies holding government contracts were Sheriff James Pease and his partner Henry L. Hertz, who served as Coroner, State Treasurer, and Chicago Internal Revenue Collector; Fred Busse, Chicago Postmaster 1905–07 and Mayor 1907–11; and Fred U. Upham, Illinois National Committeeman and member of the Cook County Board of Review, who was a partner with Francis S. Peabody, Sheriff and Democratic National Committeeman. In the bonding business were Republicans James L. Monaghan, deputy County Comptroller and a leading Lorimer lieutenant, Fred Blount, Twentieth Ward County Committeeman (partners with United States Senator Albert J. Hopkins), and Democratic powers George Brennan, John McGillen (Secretary of the Cook County Democratic Committee), and Congressman Adolph Sabath.

Construction companies were also considered a profitable sideline. Lorimer had two: the Lorimer & Gallagher Construction Company and the Federal Improvement Company. Sullivan and Hopkins controlled the Chicago and Great Lakes Dredging and Dock Company. Thomas Gahan, a member of the Sullivan-Hopkins faction and Democratic County Chairman in the 1890's, was a partner in the Gahan and Byrne Construction Company. And Hopkins was involved through his nephew with the Lyden and Drews Construction Company. These politically connected firms held a large share of the contracts for the building and maintenance of Chicago's drainage canal. In the fourteen years from 1890–1914, Lyden and Drews held contracts totaling $1,393,902; Gahan and Byrne, $1,186,136; Chicago and Great Lakes Dredging and Dock, $620,318; and the Lorimer firms, $280,746. Lorimer was also president of the Murphy-Lorimer Brick Company (Murphy was a Democratic alderman) which sold brick to the Sanitary and Park Districts. Martin Madden, a Chicago Republican alderman of the "gray wolf" variety who later served creditably in Congress, was president of the Western Stone Company which supplied the city and county with street and building materials.

A more complicated form of political entrepreneurship is revealed by the Ogden Gas Company. Roger C. Sullivan was president and the principal stockholders included John P. Hopkins, Chairman Thomas Gahan of the Cook County Democratic Central Committee, and Democratic Alderman John C. Powers. The Sullivan-Hopkins group formed the Ogden Company in 1895 and, with the help of Republicans like Madden, pushed a liberal franchise through the City Council. The Ogden Ordinance was what was called a "mace," a measure passed for blackmail purposes. The real goal in organizing the company was not to produce gas but to force the People's Gas Light and Coke Company to buy it out at an exhorbitant price. When the People's Gas Company refused to buy, the Ogden Company actually began the production and sale of gas, stirring up intermittent price wars until the People's Company finally capitulated and made the purchase.

Political entrepreneurship is also revealed in the relationship of the bosses to banking. Republican boss Lorimer, for instance, in partnership with downstate Illinois banker Charles B. Munday opened a string of banks in 1909. Lorimer and Munday planned to obtain public deposits through Lorimer's influence. When their main bank, the LaSalle Street Bank, opened, numerous Illinois politicians were solicited to become stockholders. Among those who became either stockholders or officers, were two former Chief Clerks of the State Auditor's Office (responsible for the regulation of state banks); a state bank examiner; numerous Assemblymen;

and several members of the Cook County Republican and Democratic Central Committees. Many politicians held loans from the
Lorimer banks, some as large as $65,000.

Through the influence of their politician directors and stockholders and in spite of an unsavory reputation, the Lorimer-Munday
banks received public deposits. In 1914 when the over-extended
bank chain collapsed, the LaSalle Street Bank had $870,141 in
deposits from the city of Chicago, the Sanitary District, the Superior
and Probate Court Clerks, the State Auditor, and in federal postal
savings funds; this represented approximately 26 percent of the
bank's total deposits. Several other Lorimer-Munday banks also held
public deposits.

The same type of political banking setup, although on a far more
extensive scale, involved the John R. Walsh banks of Chicago.
Walsh was an Irish immigrant who became an important Chicago
businessman-banker. He controlled the Chicago National Bank, the
Home Savings Company, and the Equitable Trust Company. He
owned, at various times, several newspapers including the *Chicago
Chronicle,* and the *Herald,* controlled several railroads, and was a
director of numerous corporations. The Walsh banks, which were
the center of his economic interests since Walsh invested bank
funds in his own corporations, were unique in that they were
political banks. During the 1890's and through 1905, they held large
deposits from Chicago, the Sanitary District, the various park
boards, Cook County, and the state. Depending upon the time of
the year, the total of public funds in the Walsh banks varied between
four and thirteen million dollars, a large part of their total holdings.

Walsh secured the public funds through his close relationships
with the two political machines. Sullivan and Hopkins were both
large stockholders in the Chicago National, as was Andrew J.
Graham, the Sullivan-Hopkins candidate for mayor in 1911. The chief
contacts with the Lorimer organization were Fred M. Blount, vice-
president of the Chicago National, and John M. Smyth, a millionaire
furniture distributor and director of that bank. Both Blount and
Smyth were businessmen-politicians. They were close friends of
Lorimer and divided their time between their firms, the several
wards they controlled, and service on the Cook County Republican

Central Committee, of which Smyth served as chairman several times.

Through his political allies, Walsh obtained appointments for his bank officials to positions with control over public funds. He himself served as treasurer of the Chicago South Park Board from 1888–1905, while William Best, a director of the Chicago National, and Lyman C. Walton, vice-president of the Equitable Trust, comprised the rest of the board. Blount was treasurer of the West Park Board (on which Andrew Graham also sat) in 1888–94 and 1897–1905, and of the Chicago Sanitary District during 1896–1906. The three Walsh banks held most of the public funds from these governmental bodies.

A number of Chicago politicians held loans from the Walsh banks. While it was not unusual for politicians to borrow money, the number involved suggests that there was a relationship between the loans and the large public deposits held by the Walsh banks. All the politicians who were stockholders or officers in the Chicago National borrowed large sums. In 1905, the only year for which records are available, John M. Smyth held a total of $475,000, Fred M. Blount, $28,500, A. J. Graham, $30,000, John P. Hopkins, $50,000, and Roger C. Sullivan, $15,000. Other politicians who were borrowers from the Walsh banks included then Postmaster Fred Busse, $46,500; Judge Elbridge Hanecy, Lorimer's candidate for governor in 1900 and mayor in 1901, $46,000; Charles U. Gordon, Chicago Postmaster from 1897–1901, $20,000; and Joseph C. Braden, Republican Sanitary District Trustee, $19,000. Lorimer's business partner James P. Gallagher owed $20,000 and Lorimer's coal company, O'Gara King, $72,094. A number of other Chicago politicians were indebted for sums under $10,000.

The Walsh and Lorimer political-banking systems and the other examples of political entrepreneurship engaged in by Chicago politicians reveals the extent to which professional politicians used their political influence as a wedge to secure economic gain. They agreed with Plunkitt that "when a man works in politics, he should get something out of it." Of course, this has always been true of American politicians to an extent, but seldom have the opportunities for entrepreneurship been as available as in turn-of-the-century Ameri-

can cities. And one might add, as sanctioned by the social environment. As Lord Bryce noted, the bosses were "the offspring of a
system. Their morality is that of their surroundings."

The widespread existence and acceptance of political entrepreneurship, however, does not mean that there were no limitations
upon the politicians. Efficiency-minded reformers were disturbed
by the waste and graft of the system. Those who held "Yankee"
ideas of morality and public responsibility looked with abhorrence
upon such activities, especially in regard to gambling, vice and
liquor. And other, more tolerant observers, while not objecting to
the politician making money out of politics, insisted that he make it
honestly, giving full measure for payment.

Many of the attacks made upon political machines and bosses
during the progressive period were directed against the private use
of politics. Municipal reformers, often coming from elite Protestant
backgrounds, sought power in order to apply their standards of
morality and corporate models of efficiency to the urban environment. Machine politicians understandably fought these attempts to
oust them from power, as did their followers, who resented reform
programs as attacks upon their life-styles. Many voters accepted it
as natural that the politician make something from his profession;
they were suspicious of those that didn't. In turn, they expected
concrete returns from politics and government. Thus, the political
boss and his machine followers, like their business allies, shared in
the largesse of an industrializing society and took advantage of the
opportunities presented by expanding urban America.

# III BOSSES AND REFORMERS

*Richard C. Wade*

# THE PERIPHERY VERSUS THE CENTER

*According to Richard C. Wade, when the boss and his machine clashed with urban reformers during the Progressive era, it was a battle between the inner city and the city's outlying residential neighborhoods. The older middle-class residents of urban America, who had taken advantage of the transportation revolution of the late nineteenth century to move to the city's more spacious outskirts, were represented in reform associations. Conversely, the machine championed the interests of the newly arrived immigrants who crowded into the core city wards. The two groups struggled to determine which would shape the life of the metropolis. While studying this periphery-versus-center model for urban politics, the student might consider what alternative models exist. Professor Wade is a scholar in the field of American urban history and has authored, among other works,* The Urban Frontier *and* Slavery in the Cities.

This new city refashioned American society and increasingly dominated national affairs. Not only were immigrants from abroad attracted to it, but young people from the farms and country were also caught in the urban undertow. The census takers, of course, could measure quantitatively the numerical shift from country to city, but the novelist Harold Frederic saw the change on a more sensitive gauge. "The nineteenth century is a century of cities," he wrote bitterly. "They have given then one twist to the progress of the age—and the farmer is as far out of it as if he lived in Alaska. Perhaps there was a time when a man could live in what the poet calls daily communication with nature and not starve his mind or dwarf his soul, but this isn't the century." The end of rural supremacy, symbolized by the searing discontent of the Populists, took place long before the census bureau counted over half the people living in "urban places"—a watershed not reached until 1920.

Indeed, the conflicts within the new urban society soon displaced the old city versus country antagonism. For the metropolis had its own divisions. The process of growth had divided the city. The newcomers appropriated the inner city, in areas where people were

Reprinted from Section IV of Chapter 14, "Urbanization," by Richard C. Wade in *The Comparative Approach to American History*, edited by C. Vann Woodward, © 1968 by C. Vann Woodward, Basic Books, Inc., Publishers, New York.

afflicted with great congestion, irregular jobs, and pervasive and persistent poverty. Strangers in a new land and new environment, they struggled to keep some kind of social organization and identity. None of their old institutions seemed wholly relevant to their new predicament; but they utilized what they could, and through voluntary associations they met some of their important needs. Still the newcomers remained economically weak and socially insecure.

But they found some protection in numbers. These numbers were in most cases a curse; housing never caught up with demand, the job market was always flooded, the breadwinner had too many mouths to feed. Yet in politics such a liability could be turned into an asset. If the residents could be mobilized, their combined strength would be able to do what none could do alone. Soon the "boss" and the "machine" arose to organize this potential. Feeding on the vulnerability of the neighborhoods and the hostility of the outside world, the boss system became a distinctive feature of American politics. It succeeded because it was rooted in the realities of block life—the clubhouse, the saloon, the cheap theaters, and the street. Moreover, it met certain specific needs. The boss helped recent arrivals to find housing, secured them jobs, mediated with public authorities, managed families through bad times, and somehow gave the recent arrivals a sense of belonging to their new land. To be sure, the cost was not small—laws were bent and broken; officials corrupted; funds embezzled; the franchises sullied. Essentially, however, the boss system was simply the political expression of inner city life.

Conditions, were, however, much different in the pleasant residential areas which ringed the new city. Here the residents lived in detached houses on large lots or in new two- or three-story flats within commuting distance to downtown. Neighborhood life revolved around churches, schools, and voluntary societies. The men hurried for the streetcar every morning and joined the business and professional life of the expanding city. Political organization in these white-collar residential areas was as much an expression of the neighborhood as the boss system was of the congested center. "Reform associations" grew up to protect and advance the concerns of the middle-class constituents of the outlying wards. Thus the characteristic instrument of reform was "the committee of one hundred," or the "committee of seventy-five," etc. Since the neighborhoods were scattered and the interests diverse, unlike the more compact and monolithic center, the periphery found the broadly based committee more appropriate than the "boss."

As the machine scored increasing successes around the country in what one writer described as "the Irish captivity of American cities," reform groups gathered forces in an effort to reclaim the city. Initially, urban reform centered on an attempt to clean up municipal corruption and to find some better means of coming to grips with a wide range of pressing local problems. Only later was this impulse translated into a national movement. The enemy of this civic uprising, of course, was the city boss and his machine. Local business interests which had working arrangements with this political system also came under attack, especially traction magnates, gas rings, and utilities companies. The connection between "bad" politics and "bad" business became one of the most significant problems for urban reformers; indeed, little was said later by national progressives on this question that had not already been argued in the metropolis. But in the municipal context, the central target was the boss and his control of city hall.

The drive for improvement began sporadically in the seventies; toward the end of the century reform administrations appeared with increasing frequency. Though this municipal agitation contributed to the general discontent of the period, it grew independently of the rural protest embodied in Granger and Populist activity. It addressed itself to different objectives. Moreover, when the agrarian revolt failed in 1896 and new conditions calmed the countryside, urban reform activity continued at an accelerated pace. The years between the failure of Bryan and the accession of Theodore Roosevelt, so often left dangling awkwardly between Populism and Progressivism, were in fact filled with significant successes on the municipal level. When the twentieth century opened, the basis for a new surge of national liberalism was present in cities all across the country.

Progressivism in this phase was an intra-urban conflict, and, although not without economic overtones, it was essentially political. Reform found its major spokesmen and greatest support in middle-class residential areas on the outer ring of the city. These were the wards occupied by the older inhabitants who had abandoned downtown for the more pleasant, less congested spots. Ethnically these sections were white and heavily Protestant. The boss's strength was in the city's core where the newcomers had settled. These were the tenement, tenderloin, and transient precincts. Low income, irregular employment, and overcrowding prevailed. The people were predominantly immigrants; neighborhoods developed strong ethnic flavorings; large proportions of the residents were Catholic or Jewish. Hence, reform was a movement of the periphery against the center.

The two camps divided over many questions. The formal issues usually had to do with "charter reform" and attempts to change existing structures of municipal government. But the real cleavage went much deeper. The contest was to determine whether the oldest residents or the newcomers would shape the life of the metropolis. Behind the attack on the boss lay thinly disguised hostility to the hyphenated population of the central city. The drive for a civil service system always carried an implied attack on immigrant leaders and their modest educational qualifications for public office. Charges of corruption in city hall, whether true or not, usually suggested that the natives and foreign-born had different standards of conduct and honesty. And the sporadic raids on vice and gambling, generally directed at saloons and beer halls, carried a judgment on the private habits of the downtown neighborhoods.

The attack usually strengthened the boss and the machine, permitting them to pose as the protectors of oppressed segments of the city's life and the defenders of persecuted minorities. Nor was this wholly a pose. At a time when others preached self-help and limited government, the boss practiced paternalism and municipal service. People in his area felt they needed help—getting housing, jobs, relief, leniency in court judgment, even exemptions from the law. Reformers thought assistance in these fields was harmful both to those who received and to the public agency that provided it. The boss had no such inhibitions. He did what he could, and when successful he expected recipients to show their gratitude by supporting him. When a city-wide showdown came, they seldom disappointed him. To the people of the neighborhood he had become a symbol of both their predicament and their hope. His enemies were somehow theirs; his triumphs would also be theirs.

Political patterns in the Progressive era reflected this split between the middle of the city and its outer edges. Voting results could be plotted on a map; reform majorities dwindled, then disappeared, as they crossed over the lines demarcating the oldest parts of town. The balance between the forces was close enough to afford victories for both sides and to make no defeat permanent. In the first decades, reform succeeded often enough to make improvements in municipal government. Boss rule, however, was so deeply rooted in the needs of the neighborhood and the requirements of newcomers that it could only be tamed, not killed. Yet the battle itself had led to a valuable discussion of city problems. The competence of local government was greatly widened and the standards of municipal service measurably raised.

These internal urban political struggles had a broad significance for national Progressivism. Reformers active in local affairs often moved onto a wider stage, and they carried the same attitudes into the national arena that informed their approach to municipal problems. Hence, Progressivism found it difficult to appeal to the crowded center of the cities. Historians have observed, usually with some surprise, that neither labor nor immigrant groups responded very enthusiastically to progressive programs or leaders. The answer to this riddle is not only that Progressivism was essentially a middle-class movement, but also that it was led by the same people whose local activities had been directed against the residents of the downtown neighborhoods. Having rejected such leadership in the city, tenement dwellers could scarcely be expected to embrace it in the nation.

The gap between the center and the periphery remained a constant factor in local and national affairs for nearly three decades. The first major figure to build a bridge across this chasm was Alfred E. Smith of New York. Himself a product of the tenement and immigration section, he had a claim on the support of the machine; but he also developed strong ties with the reform community. His extraordinarily successful career in New York reflected an ability to join the traditional antagonists. What Smith accomplished within one state, Franklin Roosevelt was able to accomplish on a national scale. Standing prominently in the famous New Deal coalition were the boss and the reformer, neither exactly comfortable, but together making very formidable what political scientists came to call the "urban consensus."

*Zane L. Miller*

# BOSS COX'S CINCINNATI

*With some modification, Zane L. Miller applies Wade's model to a specific city, Cincinnati. There Miller finds that Boss George H. Cox helped impose order on a city disorganized by its transformation from a mid-nineteenth century walking city to a modern fragmented metropolis. Divided into three zones, the Circle, the Zone, and the Hilltops, Boss Cox's Cincinnati exemplified the concentric circle model of urban development. Although first organizing the periphery to oppose the center, Cox lost power when he brought the inner city into his coalition. The Hilltop reformers, although building upon the changes achieved by the boss and his allies, turned against them, unable to accept a working relationship with the inner-city masses. The boss, nevertheless, had brought reform to his city. Professor Miller gives an in-depth account in* Boss Cox's Cincinnati: Urban Politics in the Progressive era.

Many observers of the turn-of-the-century urban scene have depicted bossism as one of the great unmitigated evils of the American city, as a tyrannical, authoritarian, relentlessly efficient and virtually invulnerable political system. Between 1904 and 1912, for example, George B. Cox was castigated by writers in four national magazines. Gustav Karger called him the "Proprietor of Cincinnati." Lincoln Steffens declared that "Cox's System" was "one great graft," "the most perfect thing of the kind in this country." Frank Parker Stockbridge claimed that "The Biggest Boss of Them All" had an organization "more compact and closely knit than any of the political machines which have dominated New York, Philadelphia, Chicago, St. Louis or San Francisco." And George Kibbe Turner concluded that in the 1890s "the man from Dead Man's

Reprinted by permission of the Organization of American Historians from Zane L. Miller, "Boss Cox's Cincinnati: A Study in Urbanization and Politics, 1880–1914," *Journal of American History*, LIV (March 1968), pp. 823–838.

Corner . . . seated himself over the city of Cincinnati. For twenty years he remained there—a figure like no other in the United States, or in the world." Yet these knowledgeable and sensitive journalists obscured as much as they revealed about the nature of Queen City politics in the Progressive era. A new kind of city had developed, and "the boss" comprised only a fraction of its novel political system.

Paradoxically, Cox and his machine were produced by, fed on, and ultimately helped dispel the spectacular disorder which engulfed Cincinnati in the late-nineteenth century and threatened the very survival of the democratic political process. In these years, increasing industrialization, technological innovations in communication and transportation—especially the coming of rapid transit—and continued foreign and domestic migration had reversed the physical pattern of the mid-century walking city and transformed Cincinnati into a physically enlarged, divided, and potentially explosive metropolis.

\*     \*     \*

The fashionable residential districts which had flanked the center of the walking city began to disintegrate. One family after another fled the East End for the hills around the Basin, leaving only a small coterie led by the Charles P. Tafts to stave off the advance of factories and slums. The elite West End seemed to disappear overnight. It "did not go down imperceptibly," recalled one old resident. "It went to ruin almost as if a bombshell sent it to destruction."

The Hilltops, at mid-century the private preserve of cemeteries, colleges, and a handful of wealthy families, became the prime residential district in the new city. The crush to get in generated new tensions. . . .

The diffusion of wealthy families, the reduction in casual social and business contacts, and the construction of new communities made ardent joiners of the Hilltops elite. Each neighborhood had an improvement association, and between 1880 and 1905 five new businessmen's organizations devoted to boosting the city's lethargic economy had appeared. In the same period six social clubs opened downtown facilities, and three country clubs were started. By 1913, moreover, there were twenty-two exclusive clubs and patriotic societies and innumerable women's groups. These developments helped counteract the disruptive effects of the "country movement," as one visitor labeled it, which was "so general that church-going became an affair of some difficulty" and "society itself . . . more or less disintegrated."

But not all those moving out were affluent. Liberated by rapid transit, skilled and semiskilled workers and moderately prosperous professional and white-collar men with life savings, the courage to take out a mortgage, an equity in a building and loan association, or a willingness to rent a flat in a double or triple decker, also fled the Basin. They took refuge in a no-man's-land between the center of the city and the Hilltops frontier which was similar to an area dubbed the Zone of Emergence by Boston social workers.

Zone residents formed what the Cincinnati *Post* referred to as "the so-called middle class . . . , the class that makes any city . . . what it is . . . [,] the class that takes in the great body of people between wealth and poverty" and builds up "many organizations, societies, associations, fraternities and clubs that bring together people who are striving upward, trying to uplift themselves, and hence human society."

*       *       *

The exodus, however, did not depopulate the Basin. Instead, a great residential Circle formed around the central business district. It filled with newcomers and those who lacked the means to get out —rural whites and Negroes from the South, Germans, Irish, Greeks, Italians, and Jews from eastern Europe. Working at the poorest paying jobs available, they were jammed into the most congested quarters. The Circle led all other areas of the city in arrests, mortality, and disease.

Although the pressure to escape was enormous, the barriers were formidable. Ignorant of the ways of the city, as an Associated Charities report put it, Circle dwellers had to be "shown how to buy, how to cook, how to make the home attractive, how to find employment." Many, "utterly friendless and discouraged," succumbed to "the damnable absence of want or desire" and grew "indifferent . . . to their own elevation." Plagued by "physical bankruptcy," they found it difficult to find and hold jobs, let alone form and maintain the kind of organizations which enabled Zone residents to shield themselves from economic disaster, legal pitfalls, social isolation, and apathy.

The immediate impact of the emergence of the new city pushed Cincinnati to the brink of anarchy. In March 1884, the *Enquirer* complained that the police had failed to choke off a crime wave although, in the last year alone, there had been twelve arrests for malicious shooting, twenty-nine for malicious cutting, forty-seven for cutting with intent to wound, 284 for shooting with intent to kill, ninety-two for murder and manslaughter, and 948 for carrying a concealed weapon. The total number of arrests came to 56,784. The city's population was 250,000. Later that same month, a lynch mob descended on the county jail. While police and militia fought off the mob, gangs looted stores and shops on the fringe of the downtown district. In three days of riot the courthouse was burned to the ground, fifty-four people were killed, and an estimated 200 people wounded.

During the fall elections, violence erupted in the lower wards; two policemen and one Negro were killed. Congressman Benjamin Butterworth remarked that he had "never witnessed anywhere such coarse brutality and such riotous demonstrations. . . ." Cincinnati, he concluded, "seems . . . doomed to perdition."

Less than two years later the city faced another major crisis. On May 1, 1886, Cincinnati workers joined in nationwide demonstrations for the eight-hour day. These were followed by a series of strikes. The militia was called out, and for two weeks the city resembled an armed camp. Only the show of force and, perhaps, the memory of the courthouse catastrophe prevented another riot.

Yet labor remained restive, and a rash of strikes followed. By 1892, the paternalistic system which had dominated the breweries was smashed. And in 1894, Judge William Howard Taft spent the hot days of June and July "trying to say nothing to reporters" and "issuing injunctions" in an effort to control and prevent the railroad strike from leading to mass violence.

The Sunday-closing question was another explosive issue. The *Post,* the *Catholic-Telegraph,* a Committee of Five Hundred, and many Protestant clergymen all leveled scathing attacks on the continental Sabbath. "Sunday in Cincinnati," asserted one Methodist

minister, "is a high carnival of drunkenness, base sensuality, reek-
ing debauchery and bloody, often fatal crime." Other spokesmen
tied the open Sunday to anarchism, atheism, corrupt politicians, a
decadent daily press, indifferent public officials, and the ruthless
exploitation of labor. "The modern Puritan," insisted Charles P.
Taft, "intends to rise up and oppose to the uttermost this kind of
Sunday."

When, in 1889, the mayor announced his intention to enforce the
Sunday-closing law for saloons, the city almost faced another riot.
Some 1,000 saloonkeepers vowed to ignore the new policy. When
a cadre of police and firemen marched over the Rhine to close
Kissell's saloon, an unruly crowd gathered, epithets were hurled,
but no violence occurred. Kissell's was closed; the "era of the back
door," with "front doors locked and curtains up, but back doors
widened," had opened.

These spectacular outbreaks plus other pressures overwhelmed
city hall. Indeed, scarcely a residential area, economic interest, or
social or occupational group was left unscathed by the multidimen-
sional disorder. As the physical area of the city expanded, officials
were besieged by demands for the extension, improvement, and
inauguration of public services of all kinds and for lower taxes.
Simultaneously, the relative decline of the city heightened the
urgency of the agitation. Municipal institutions and agencies, established to meet the needs of the walking city, became overburdened,
outmoded, and dilapidated.

The new city, with old ways shattered, provided a fertile breeding
ground for turmoil and discontent and, as it turned out, for innova-
tion and creative reconstruction. Initially, however, this unprecedented change accompanied by unprecedented demands for government action produced only the hope of reform. In 1885, on the eve
of the repudiation of a Democratic administration, William Howard
Taft predicted that "the clouds are beginning to break over this
Sodom of ours and the sun of decency is beginning to dispel the
moral miasma that has rested on us now for so many years. It's the
beginning of an era of reform."

Yet for almost a decade no party could put together a decisive
ruling majority. The city's political processes seemed frozen by a
paralyzing factionalism. The division of the city into residential

districts which roughly coincided with socio-economic lines made it difficult for the wealthy and well-educated to keep in contact with and control ward politics. As a result, extreme factionalism developed which could, apparently, be surmounted only by appealing to a host of neighborhood leaders and by constructing alliances which crossed party lines.

According to close observers, the chief products of this system were the use of money in city conventions and the rise of what Charles P. Taft called the "bummer," a "queer creature" who "evolves somehow from the slums. . . ." In youth "a bootblack, a newsboy or a general loafer," he matured into "an Arab" who needed only "a good standing with a saloon that has a fine layout during the day." A "hustler at the polls and conventions," the bummer was in such demand that he could accept money from competing candidates, thus lengthening the convention and contributing to interfactional dealing. After studying the influence of the "bummer," Taft gloomily concluded that the "day of pure politics can never be . . . until a riot, a plague or flood kills off all the ward bummers."

By 1897, however, and without divine intervention, all this had changed. In January of that year, three months before the city election, the *Post* gravely announced its intention to describe "impassionately and without bias the means employed" in Cincinnati's "superior and unrecorded government." It was controlled by "the boss, whose power is absolute"—George B. Cox.

The *Post*'s analysis closely paralleled those made after the turn of the century. It dissected the patronage system, outlined the sources of financial support, and noted the attempted appeasement of the city's various special groups—the soldiers, the Germans, the Republican clubs, the Reform Jews, the legal and medical professions, the socially prominent Hilltops businessmen, and certain cooperative Democrats. It excitedly reported the effectiveness of the organization's intelligence system, the way the "plugger" and the "knocker" wore "beaten paths to the office of the boss to urge the appointment of this man, the discharge of that [,] or to report some feature of misconduct or expression. . . ." The paper noted that Cox was always available for consultation with any citizen regardless of station or status and that he had been little more than one of several important factional leaders until, in 1886, Governor Joseph B. Foraker selected him to serve as chief adviser on patronage and political affairs in Hamilton County.

Foraker made a shrewd choice; Cox had grown up with the new city and received a liberal education in its ways. The son of British immigrants he was born in 1853 and reared in the Eighteenth Ward, a district which by the 1880's contained fashionable as well as slum housing, factories, and its share of saloons and brothels. His father died when Cox was eight. Successively, Cox worked as a bootblack, newsboy, lookout for a gambling joint, grocery deliveryman, bartender, and tobacco salesman. His school principal, who later became superintendent of schools, claimed that Cox was frequently in boyish trouble in classes, exhibited an "undisguised love for his mother," and "never lied . . . bore malice, sulked, whined or moped." Cox had also been exposed to religion. Although not a churchgoer, as an adult he had, according to one journalist, "dormant powerful sentiments, which rest on foundations of the firmest faith."

In the mid-1870s Cox acquired a saloon in his home neighborhood. He entered politics and served on the city council from 1878 until 1885 when, after joining forces with the Republican reform mayoralty candidate, he ran unsuccessfully for county clerk. He tried for the same post in 1888, failed, and never again stood for public office.

At that time, moving away politically from the Circle, Cox worked with George Moerlein, perhaps the strongest of the GOP professionals in the Zone. In 1890, he and Moerlein quarreled over patronage; and in the city convention of 1891, Cox was able, with the support of the Blaine Club, a kind of political settlement house that he had helped to establish, to defeat Moerlein's candidate for police judge and nominate his own man. Moerlein men now became Cox men. So, too, did Charles P. Taft and the *Times-Star,* which had been one of the last, the most influential, and the most outspoken of Cox's critics in the Hilltops Republican ranks. It accepted Cox, the paper announced, to secure a "New Order" for Cincinnati. And the president of the gas company, sensing the political drift, confided to his diary that he had "concluded [an] arrangement with Geo. B. Cox for services at $3500 per year quarterly to last for three years." In the spring election of 1894 the Republicans carried the city with a plurality of over 6,500 votes, the first decisive municipal election in a decade. In 1897, Cox was the honest broker in a coalition composed of Circle and Zone Negroes, Zone politicians, the gas and traction companies, and Hilltops Republican reformers.

Election returns after 1885 disclose a clear pattern. The GOP won five successive contests by uniting powerful Hilltops support with enough strength in the Zone to overcome the Democratic grip on the Circle. Until 1894 the margins of victory were perilously thin. The substantial triumph of that year merely marked the completion of the alliance which pitted a united periphery against the center of the city.

The heart of the Republican "New Order" coalition, and the critical factor in the election of 1894, was its appeal to voters in the Hilltops fringe who demanded order and reform. To satisfy the Hilltops, Cox and his associates eliminated the bummer, provided brief and decorous conventions, enfranchised Negroes by suppressing violence at the polls, reduced the rapid turnover in office, and cut down the incidence of petty graft and corporation raiding.

Moreover, the "machine" heeded the advice of its reform allies from the Hilltops. Cox accepted the secret ballot, voter registration, and a series of state laws which, though retaining the mayor-council form of government with ward representation, were designed to give the city a stable and more centralized government. The administrations which he indorsed started to build a professional police force, expanded and reequipped the fire department, pushed through a $6,000,000 water-works program, renovated municipal institutions, supported the growth of the University of Cincinnati, launched extensive street-paving and sewer-construction projects, and tried to reduce the smoke problem and expand the city's park acreage. They also opened the door to housing regulation, suppressed the Sunday saloon, flagrant public gambling, and disorderly brothels (the city was never really closed), began to bring order into the chaotic public-utilities field by favoring privately owned, publicly regulated monopolies under progressive management, and succeeded in keeping the tax rate low. The Republican regime, in short, brought positive government to Cincinnati.

While this program also won votes in the Zone, it was not the sole basis for the party's popularity there. Many of the lieutenants and captains closest to Cox were Zone residents. They composed a colorful group known variously as "the gang," "the sports," or the "bonifaces"—a clique which met nightly Over-the-Rhine either at Schubert and Pels, where each had a special beer mug with his name gilded on it, or at the round table in Wielert's beer garden. Three of them owned or operated combination saloons, gambling joints, and dance halls; one was prominent in German charitable associations and the author of several textbooks used in the elementary schools; another served twenty consecutive terms as president of the Hamilton County League of Building Associations; and one was a former catcher for the Cincinnati Redlegs.

Their tastes, behavior, and attitudes were conveniently summarized in the biographical sketches of ward leaders and city officials in the 1901 *Police and Municipal Guide.* All were characterized as friendly, well-known, "All Around Good-Fellows" who liked a story, belonged to several social and fraternal groups, gave generously to charity, and treated the poor and sick with special kindness. They were all among the most ardent supporters of any project to boost the city.

Cox is pictured in the *Guide* as an adherent to the code of the Zone who had risen to the top. He was a *bon vivant* who enjoyed good cigars and good jokes, a man of wealth whose recently completed Clifton mansion was luxuriously decorated and adorned with expensive works of art, a man of impressive but quiet and private charity. Above all, he was true to his word, loyal to his friends, yet quick to reprimand and replace those who betrayed his trust by misusing public office.

Cox and his top civil servants—surrounded by a motley crowd of newspaper reporters, former boxers and ball players, vaudeville and burlesque performers, and other Vine Street characters—provided an attractive model for men awed by the glamor, wealth, and power which was so visible yet so elusive in the new city. Cox's opponents in the Zone seldom attacked him or this inside group directly. Even in the heat of the 1897 campaign, the *Volksfreund,* the German Catholic Democratic daily, carefully described Cox as an "amiable man" who had to be "admired" for his "success" and, either ignoring or unaware of the process of negotiation and mediation by which he ruled, criticized him only for his illiberality in imposing "dictatorial methods" on the GOP. Indeed, most Zone residents, like those of the Hilltops, found it difficult to object to a government which seemed humane, efficient, and progressive.

Yet it would be a mistake to overestimate the strength of the "New Order" Republican coalition. Its victories from 1885 to 1894 were won by perilously close pluralities. The organization, moreover, failed to carry a referendum for the sale of the city-owned Southern Railroad in 1896 and lost the municipal contest in 1897 to a reform fusion ticket, and the fall elections of 1897, 1898, and 1899 to the Democrats. In all these reversals, crucial defections occurred in both the Hilltops and the Zone. Skittish voters grew indignant over alleged corruption, outraged by inaction on the traction and gas questions, piqued by the rising cost of new city projects, annoyed by the slow expansion of the educational program, or uneasy over the partial sacrifice of democracy to efficiency within the Republican organization.

Thereafter, however, the Republicans rallied and won three of the next four city elections by unprecedented margins. The strategy and tactics remained essentially the same. Although not wholly averse to raising national issues, Cox's group gave local affairs the most emphasis. The organization was occasionally purged of its less savory elements. Cox and his Zone advisors continued to consult with their Hilltops allies on nominations. The party promised and, in fact, tried to deliver order and reform. Without abolishing ward representation in the city council, it strengthened the mayor and streamlined the administration. The party also broadened and deepened its program as civic associations, women's clubs, social workers, social gospellers, and spokesmen for the new unionism—all novel forces in urban politics—expanded and elaborated their demands.

But voting patterns underwent a fundamental and, for the GOP, an ultimately disastrous change. By 1903 the Republicans dominated the entire city, carrying not only the Zone and Hilltops but also the center. The Circle was now the invincible bulwark of Cox's power.

There were several factors involved in the conversion of Circle Democrats to Republicanism. First, Cox had extensive personal contacts with them which dated back to his unsuccessful races for county clerk in the 1880s. Second, the Democrats had been unable to put down factionalism. By the late 1890s there were two reform elements in the party, both of which belabored the regulars from the center of the city as tainted with corruption, too cozy with Cox, and perhaps worst of all, as a discredit and burden to the party because they wore the charred shirt of the courthouse riot.

*      *      *

It was this alliance with the Circle which ultimately destroyed Cox. Anti-machine spokesmen were convinced that they had to educate the city before they could redeem it. They felt, too, that politics was a potent educational tool. But campaigns had to be spectacular in order to engage the voters' attention and participation. As A. Julius Freiberg notes, the "psychology" of the electorate was such that years of "speaking, writing, explaining, even begging and imploring" had been "to no purpose." The "reformer and his fellow students may sit about the table and evolve high principles for action, but the people . . . will not be fed by those principles unless there is a dramatic setting, and the favorite dramatic setting is the killing of a dragon." And all the people "love the dramatic; not merely the poor, but the rich, and the middle class as well." All that was needed was a situation which would enable the right man to "bring to book the boss himself."

Reformers hammered relentlessly at the theme that Cox was not a good boss; he was the head of a "syndicate" which included the worst products of slum life. . . .

The reformers also impugned Cox's personal integrity. Democratic County Prosecutor Henry T. Hunt secured evidence that Cox had perjured himself in 1906 when he said he had not received a cent of some $250,000 of interest on public funds which Republican county treasurers had been paid by bankers. In the spring of 1911, Hunt and the grand jury indicted Cox and 123 others during a broad investigation of politics, corruption, and vice.

Finally, Hunt, stressing the issue of moral indignation, ran for mayor in the fall of 1911 on a Democratic reform ticket. Using the moral rhetoric of the muckraker, Hunt and his associates tied bossism, the chaos, poverty, and vice of the slums, and the malefactors of great wealth together and pictured them as a threat to the welfare of the whole city. Once again the Hilltops and Zone voted for order and reform. Hunt's progressive coalition swept the periphery, lost only in the Circle wards, and won the election.

By that time, however, Cox was no longer boss. President Taft and Charles P. Taft had wanted Cox to step aside as early as 1905, but they found him indispensable. After the grand jury revelations, however, they were able to convince the "bonifaces" that Cox was a liability. With the organization against him, Cox retired. For a time, he insisted that his two chief assistants, August Herrmann and Rudolph Hynicka, should also quit, apparently convinced that they, like himself, could no longer command the confidence of the periphery. Charles P. Taft's *Times-Star* agreed. The two men, backed by the Blaine Club, merely resigned their official party positions but refused to get out of politics entirely.

What, then, was Cox's role in politics and government in the new city? He helped create and manage a voluntary political-action organization which bridged the racial and cultural chasms between the Circle, Zone, and Hilltops. He and his allies were able to bring positive and moderate reform government to Cincinnati and to mitigate the conflict and disorder which accompanied the emergence of the new city. With the crisis atmosphere muted, ardent reformers could develop more sophisticated programs and agitate, educate, and organize without arousing the kind of divisive, emotional, and hysterical response which had immobilized municipal statesmen in the 1880s. In the process, while battering at the boss, the slums, and the special-privilege syndicate, they shattered the bonds of confidence which linked the Zone "bonifaces" and the moderate reformers of the Hilltops to Cox's organization. Cox, it seems, said more than he realized when, in 1892, he remarked that a boss was "not necessarily a public enemy."

*J. Joseph Huthmacher*

# BOSS MURPHY AND PROGRESSIVE REFORM

*In the following selection, Professor Huthmacher describes an urban boss operating on the state level. Charles Francis Murphy's influence extended beyond his Tammany bailiwick into the New York State legislature; much of the Progressive legislation that was passed in New York had Tammany support. Murphy, a practical politician, realized the desirability of maintaining his and the Hall's popularity with its urban working-class base by responding to their need for reform legislation. Thus Boss Murphy, like Boss Cox, often aligned himself with the advocates of reform. J. Joseph Huthmacher, a specialist in twentieth-century American history, is the author of* Massachusetts People and Politics, 1919–1933 *and* Senator Robert F. Wagner and the Rise of Urban Liberalism.

Like [Charles Evans] Hughes' life story, that of Charles F[rancis] Murphy might be fitted into a category—though of a very different kind—for Murphy's biography follows the course of a supposedly "typical" Tammany politician. Born of Irish-Catholic immigrant parents who led a poverty-stricken existence on New York's East Side, Murphy had little formal education. In his teens he worked at various odd jobs until, when twenty years old, he became a driver of a horse-drawn trolley. He managed to save five hundred dollars in two years, and then opened a saloon at East 19th Street and Avenue A. By 1890 he owned four of them. Murphy's saloons, the baseball and rowing teams he sponsored, and his fists gained him a political following, and in 1892 he became leader of his Assembly District—the Gas House District. When Boss Richard Croker resigned the Tammany leadership under a cloud of scandal in 1902, the Gas House spokesman became the chieftain of Tammany Hall.

During the first few years of Murphy's regime the Hall's character seemed to vary little from the sinister pattern established by Croker and earlier leaders. It was widely suspected—though never proved —that Murphy reaped a harvest of "honest graft," and some that

Reprinted by permission of the New York State Historical Association and the author from J. Joseph Huthmacher, "Charles Evans Hughes and Charles Francis Murphy: The Metamorphosis of Progressivism," *New York History*, XLIV (January 1965), pp. 28–34.

was not so honest, for himself and other "insiders." Moreover, in New York City and at Albany the Hall's legislative policies seemed to remain under the domination of conservative advisors who surrounded the Boss: corporation lawyers like Daniel Cohalan, Morgan J. O'Brien, and John D. Stanchfield, and business tycoons like Thomas Fortune Ryan and Anthony Brady.

On the other hand, during the Hughes administration [as Governor of New York, 1907–1910] a younger band of Tammanyites, with a somewhat deviationist view toward machine politics, began to contest with the conservative advisors for Murphy's ear. Men like Robert F. Wagner, Alfred E. Smith, Jeremiah T. Mahoney, James A. Foley (who was to become the Boss' son-in-law), and James A. Walker pleaded that "a political party couldn't remain static." Unlike Croker and the others, Murphy entertained what one writer has denoted a "grudging admiration" for a certain degree of independence among his subjects. He tolerated the deviationism of his "young men," as he called them; he encouraged them, and sent them to the legislature.

As muckraking journals like Pulitzer's *New York World* and Hearst's *New York American*—the newspapers read most widely by the city masses—stepped up their attacks on a reactionary Tammany Hall, and as the number of Socialists multiplied on the street corners of New York, distributing revolutionary literature among Tammany's constituents, the Boss became more attentive to the new currents of thought which were seeking recognition in his organization. The same effect resulted from the recurrent attacks launched against Murphy's position as his party's state leader—attacks mounted by upstate Democratic spokesmen like Thomas Mott Osborne and a young fellow named Franklin Roosevelt. The fact that an avowed reformer like Hughes could lead the Republicans to victory, even though he had helped expose the G.O.P.'s malodorous record under his immediate predecessors, also impressed Murphy. And each time the Hall suffered a setback at the polls, as it did in the municipal elections of 1909, for example, the Boss seemed to become more attuned to his young men's ideas.

To those who followed legislative news and legislative roll calls closely, the change that was beginning to take place in the Hall might have been noticed already during the Hughes regime. Though resistance to structural reform – support of social reform

Tammany legislators resisted most of Hughes' tinkerings with the political machinery, all but a handful of the most reactionary of them voted in favor of his business, labor, and welfare measures.

When the Democrats took control of the state's government in 1911, for four years as it turned out to be, Boss Murphy faced his great test. He pleased reformers by making Bob Wagner majority leader of the Senate, and Al Smith leader of the Assembly. But even with such promising leadership, the Tammany lawmakers indulged in some hi-jinks reminiscent of the old days. A flood of patronage and so-called "ripper" bills passed, creating new positions and removing Republicans from lucrative appointive jobs so as to make places for "deserving" Democrats. Even more damaging to Tammany was the series of internal disputes that wracked the Democratic Party during its period of supremacy, and called into question its qualifications as a responsible governing agency for the state. In 1911, for example, when the time came for the legislature to elect a successor to Republican United States Senator Chauncey Depew, an insurrection against Murphy's choice for the place, waged by a group of upstate Democrats led by State Senator Franklin Roosevelt, produced an unseemly fiasco that tied up the legislature and the state's business for three months.

Most disturbing of all was the 1913 spectacle in which the Democratic legislature impeached its own Democratic governor. William Sulzer had been elected with Murphy's blessing. But he entertained presidential aspirations and, taking a cue from Woodrow Wilson, viewed a fight against his state's "bosses" as a step in the direction of the White House. Murphy was prepared for such a contingency and produced irrefutable evidence that Sulzer had falsified his statement of campaign expenditures. The Governor was convicted because of his own misdeeds. Nevertheless, the impeachment was an awesome display of naked political power—power that Charles F. Murphy was determined to retain—and it heightened the belief that Murphy had, in the words of the *New York Times,* "established himself securely as the Dictator of Democratic policies in the State." This fact, and the fear that it engendered, gave the Republicans and the "goo-goos" something to work with. In November, 1913 a Fusion ticket swept Tammany out of virtually every elective office in New York City, and in November, 1914 the G.O.P. recaptured control of the state government. For a while—it turned out again to be four years—Tammany was consigned to licking its wounds and atoning for its sins.

This was the dark side of Tammany's performance from 1911 through 1914—peak years in America's Progressive Era. But there was another and brighter side to that performance—one which many people at the time, and since then, have tended to overlook. As four eminent scholars tell us in a recent history of New York State: "By 1914 New York had not reached the millenium, but it had adopted a body of forward-looking legislation that placed the state in the front ranks of the progressive movement." The great bulk of that legislation was adopted during these Democratic years, and by legislatures dominated by Wagner and Smith, two of the Tammany Boss' stand-out "young men." But as Edward J. Flynn has said, and as everybody knew, "nothing could have been done at Albany unless Charles F. Murphy permitted or encouraged it." It seems only logical, then, that the Tammany chieftain should be assigned some of the credit for advancing the Empire State toward the millenium. "Mr. Murphy," Flynn added, "has been sadly neglected in so far as progressive legislation is concerned."

The record of Democratic-approved reforms enacted between 1911 and 1914 is too extensive to bear much telling here. Although Tammany continued to drag its feet in the matter of certain types of political reform, nevertheless it did in these years become the champion of such things as woman suffrage, the direct election of United State senators, home rule for New York City and other municipalities, and even the direct primary system of nomination— measures which, according to some authorities, should have attracted no support whatsoever among the uncivic-minded people that Tammany represented. Even more impressive is the record of economic and business reform bills enacted. The Democrats pushed through ratification of the federal income-tax amendment (which Governor Hughes had opposed). They expanded the powers and scope of the State Public Utility Commission and protected its authority against adverse court decisions. The insurance, banking, and stock market industries were brought under even tighter control, and so were the cold storage and other businesses of vital concern to the consuming public. A series of measures that increased state aids to agriculture provided further evidence of the Democratic administrations' conviction that the government's role must be expanded to fit modern conditions. In the field of conservation the Democrats moved far beyond Governor Hughes' position, and committed their party to the principle of public ownership, generation, and distribution of electric energy.

[But it was in the realm of social and labor legislation, designed to ameliorate the insecurity of the state's burgeoning industrial, urban population, that the Tammany-led law-makers made their greatest contribution.] The tenement laws were safeguarded and reinforced. During this period New York launched a scholarship program for underprivileged youngsters, and a system of public employment agencies. Those who held jobs benefitted from a wide-ranging spectrum of new safety and hours regulation. The Democrats labored for a constitutional amendment authorizing compulsory workmen's compensation, and when it was secured in 1913 they enacted a compensation bill which Samuel Gompers called "the best law of the kind ever passed in any state, or in any country." The capstone of social and labor reforms in the Democratic years consisted of the accomplishments of the State Factory Investigating Commission, which was established by the legislature after the Triangle Shirtwaist Company fire of 1911 had claimed nearly 150 lives. [The Commission, of which Wagner was chairman and Smith vice-chairman, received the wholehearted support of labor unions, enlightened businessmen, social workers, and a host of middle-class civic and social reform organizations.] For four years the Commission studied the changed conditions of American life as exemplified in New York State, and its legislative members succeeded in securing enactment of fifty-seven laws designed to bring the theory and practice of social responsibility in tune with the new realities. Miss Frances Perkins has written that "The extent to which this legislation in New York marked a change in American political attitudes and policies can scarcely be overrated. It was, I am convinced, a turning point."

This record of political, economic, and social reform, which vastly overshadowed the achievements of the Hughes Administration, surely indicates that the years 1911 through 1914—years that witnessed squabbles over patronage at Albany and the impeachment of a governor—were nonetheless the peak years of New

York's Progressive Era. It clearly indicates, too, that an essential element in the compilation of that record was Tammany Hall. The fact is that during this period Charles F. Murphy, and through him the Hall as such, came to realize that there was something more to politics than ward picnics and balls. The propaganda of the Pulitzer and Hearst newspapers, and of other agitators, was gradually educating Tammany's constituents to the fact that their political strength could, if properly directed, compel the enactment of measures that would redound directly to their benefit. In response, Boss Murphy tended to give his "young men" at Albany the green light, and the more he did so, the more his constituents came to expect. The Boss and the Hall soon learned to bank on its record of support for reform measures as its most effective appeal for votes at election time, and often the results were gratifying. When the "bad" side of Tammany's record—culminating in Sulzer's impeachment—brought a stinging rebuke to the Hall in the 1913 municipal election, the Boss' conversion to his young men's viewpoint seems to have become complete. "Give the people everything they want," he is supposed to have ordered, and those orders stood during the rest of his regime as leader.]              *hard to believe !*

It is not contended of course, that the many progressive measures which New York enacted at this time were the products of Murphy's mind or of other Tammany minds, or that the Hall and its constituents deserve the sole credit (or blame) for what occurred. Usually the reform proposals originated with crusading newspapers and reform-minded organizations: labor unions, farm groups like the Grange, and numerous middle-class "professional" reform organizations such as the Citizens Union, Consumers League, Women's Trade Union League, Child Labor Committee, and the American Association for Labor Legislation. When the selfish and altruistic motives of two or more of these elements corresponded, they collaborated and worked together for adoption of their common end. Most often, sooner or later, they turned to the government, in order to achieve their reforms quickly and universally through statutory enactment. This required research and bill-drafting services, propaganda to educate the public, lobbying, and funds; these things the crusaders and their organizations provided. But their ultimate success also required that there be legislators and political leaders who were amenable to the reformers' ideas. Without them a campaign for a progressive measure would come to naught, and by no means did all politicians respond to the reformers' approaches.

New York's liberals were fortunate to have Governor Hughes heading the Republican Party for the four years 1907–1910, but thereafter control of the G.O.P. passed into the hands of the ultra-conservative, indeed reactionary, Boss William A. Barnes of Albany. Theodore Roosevelt's Bull Moose Progressive Party (which some writers tend to make the be-all and end-all of progressivism in early twentieth-century America), proved distinctly unsuccessful at the polls in New York. During its existence it elected only 3 state senators out of a possible 102, and 25 assemblymen out of a possible 600. Had the reformers' legislative success ridden upon the back of the Bull Moose, New York would have had no Progressive Era of any definable kind. After 1910, when the G.O.P. turned conservative, New York reformers relied upon the Democrats, especially upon the "younger" Tammany element, and perhaps without realizing it fully, upon Boss Charles F. Murphy himself.

[Murphy's "progressivism" was in large part the manifestation of a practical politician's self-defensive tactics. But was it, for that reason, any less worthy than the progressivism of old aristocrats or of middle-class people, displaced by a status revolution and seeking to shore up their position against a "revolution from below?" Regardless of the answer to this question, certainly the Boss' progressivism was, pragmatically, of equal importance to the cause of reform. For it signified the metamorphosis of progressivism from a rather narrowly based middle-class movement, championed originally by the minority or Hughes wing of the Republican Party, into a broader one now sustained by the powerful and permanent Democratic machine which spoke for the state's huge and growing industrial, urban, and immigrant lower-class population.]

*talks about upstate Dems (FDR) fighting w/ Tammany Dems + then lumps Dems all together*

*Melvin G. Holli*

# THE REFORMER AS MACHINE POLITICIAN

*No urban politician can succeed without an efficient organization backing him; Hazen S. Pingree, Detroit's late-nineteenth-century reform mayor, realized this. According to Melvin G. Holli, Pingree's effectiveness as a reformer was in part due to his creation of a well-disciplined political machine. In this instance, the student should consider whether there is a difference between an efficient organization and a political machine, between a boss and a "leader." Did Bosses Cox and Murphy and Mayor Pingree use similar tactics to achieve similar results? Professor Holli's work is entitled* Reform in Detroit: Hazen S. Pingree and Urban Politics.

It was Pingreeism and not Republicanism that had installed the G.O.P. in power in Detroit. When G.O.P. state and national candidates lost elections, Pingree and his municipal party won them. The Democrats swept Michigan and Wayne County in 1890, but the city Republican party won one-half of the council seats, and the Mayor went on to win re-election in 1891. The Democratic presidential and gubernatorial candidates carried Detroit and Wayne County in 1892, but Pingree added additional council seats to the G.O.P. column and registered his third victory as Mayor the next year. Throughout his career Pingree heaped abuse and recrimination upon conservative Republicans in general and upon Senator McMillan in particular. In 1894 and 1895, when the political tide was once again running with the G.O.P. in both Michigan and Wayne County, Pingree purged the council of three of its most prominent and respectable Republicans. The Mayor had broken the traditional bonds of fealty which strengthen parties and had reversed the tendency of Detroit's voters to prefer Democrats. By 1895 Pingree had almost obliterated the Democracy as a municipal party.

In a desperate attempt to make pre-Pingree political techniques work, the Democrats had thrown two former mayors, a respectable Mason, a Roman Catholic, and finally a socialist labor leader into the ring against Pingree, and all had been defeated. The party had repeated the time-honored tactic of touching upon what it believed to be every sensitive issue that motivated Detroit voters at the polls. Democratic strategy had proved faulty, however, for the party had underestimated the power of social reform.

The key to Pingree's victories after 1890 was his single-minded fight for social reform. Although clean government, honest contracts, public efficiency, and a businesslike administration never completely ceased to interest the Mayor, he increasingly came to focus his attention on issues of social reform. Theories or abstractions meant little to Pingree. He started with the observation something was fundamentally wrong with a society in which economic and political power gravitated into the hands of only a few. Although his notion was hardly original or unique in the 1890's, it is significant that he was the first large-city mayor to make a serious and sustained attempt to change that state of affairs. Clean government, low taxes, and a city-wide aldermanic system, Pingree recognized, would not redistribute economic and political power, but regulation, public ownership, trustbusting, and the transfer of the workingmen's tax burdens to previously tax-exempt corporations would. Pingree doubted that the large corporations were sharing the benefits of large-scale organization with the consumers.

Reporters observed that issues like the traction question attracted voters to Pingree, and a McMillan spoilsman pointed out that for every upper class voter the Mayor lost, he gained a "score" among the masses. The only elections which lend themselves to testing these generalizations are those of 1891 and 1893. In the former the returns showed a much higher incidence of support for the Mayor in the outer wards and precincts, which were intimately affected by the transit problem, than in the city at large. The election of 1893 clearly demonstrated a shift of upper class and native-born voters away from Pingree, but this was more than compensated for by the electoral gain achieved by the Mayor among working class and foreign-born voters. A study of the voting patterns in these elections supports the contention that it was the social reform programs espoused by the Mayor that drew votes to his support.

Although Pingree was loath to admit it, his effectiveness as an urban reformer was undoubtedly due in part to his creation of a well-disciplined political machine. Pingree used his machine to control the variety of choices that the voter had at the polls. Pingree's purges eliminated from the Republican ticket the most outspoken defenders of the utilities and business interests and anti-reform candidates and replaced them with men inclined toward the Mayor's views.

The Mayor's machine was also important in getting the faithful to the polls on election day and in insuring a uniformity of view among city employees. "I don't care a d—n about a man's politics or religion, but there's one thing I do care about, and that's his attitude toward Mayor Pingree," said Detroit Water Commissioner DeWitt Moreland. "If any man in the employ of the water board goes around abusing Mayor Pingree, or running him down, he's going to get fired—that's positive. I won't have a single Pingree-hater on the board." No "bomb throwers" would be permitted in any of the city departments, Pingree warned, in an unusual slip of candor. The Mayor noted that if any man worked for a private firm and injured the business, he would be discharged. "Now, it's the same with the city government," added Pingree. "If a man does not want to sympathize with the principles of the administration let him get a new job."

When the city's most powerful business and political interests united solidly in 1893 to defeat the Mayor, Pingree's political aides applied the powers of machine suasion more ruthlessly than they ever had before or were ever to do again. In September a new battery of health inspectors began their house-to-house canvass, and the Detroit *Free Press,* an avowed enemy of the administration, described the political manner in which the inspections were conducted:

Health inspector: *"Will you support Pingree for Mayor?"*
Householder: *"Yes sir."*
Health inspector: *"The sanitary condition of your residence is admirable, sir."*

Next Door

Health inspector: *"Do your think pretty well of Mr. Pingree for another term?"*
Householder: *"Not well enough to vote for him."*
Health inspector: *"This house is in awful shape. The sanitary conditions are enough to give the whole neighborhood Asiatic cholera. You must have a plumber here without delay."*

Although excesses of this kind were bound to occur in an administration that commanded more than 1,000 partisan employees, even Pingree's enemies conceded that there was not a single instance of thievery or corruption of the Tammany or Pendergast variety during the "Pingree era" in Detroit.

Although Pingree had no compunctions about accepting the loose ground rules of urban machine politics, he absolutely refused to tolerate dishonesty or theft. Pingree told the city convention in 1895 that he did not want "men attentive at the spigot and lax at the bung hole" but men who would advance the cause of social reform without besmirching it. Morgan Wood, a social-gospel minister, in defending the Pingree administration, explained the necessity of the Mayor's having a political organization: "The affairs of the city of Detroit can not be run without a machine; but it should be a righteous machine, well oiled to move in the interests of greatness and goodness and with the people's good always uppermost." It was, indeed, the use of machine politics to further social-reform objectives that enabled Pingree to give Detroit seven years of urban reform that were unmatched in pre-Progressive America.

*Allen F. Davis*

# THE SETTLEMENT WORKER VERSUS THE WARD BOSS

*As the earlier selection by Jane Addams indicates, the settlement-house worker often found himself competing for public support with the ward boss. Allen F. Davis relates that the success of these urban reformers often depended upon local conditions. While Miss Addams and her followers frequently were frustrated in their battles with Johnny Powers of Chicago's nineteenth ward, settlement-house workers in other areas of Chicago and Boston met with greater success. When the reformers recognized that little could be accomplished in a single ward, reform campaigns often mush-*

Adapted from *Spearheads for Reform*, pp. 148–149, 151–163, 169, by Allen F. Davis. Copyright © 1967 by Oxford University Press, Inc. Reprinted by permission.

*roomed into city-wide movements. The following selection is taken from Professor Davis' book,* Spearheads for Reform.

Most of the early settlement workers had little interest in politics when they first opened their outposts in the slums. They learned, however, that they had invaded a political world. They talked about re-creating the neighborhood in the industrial city, but they discovered that the ward and the precinct already provided a semblance of neighborhood organization and spirit. The settlement workers came to realize that for the workingman, politics was intimately connected with a job, and that any attempt to improve working and living conditions involved them in politics. In fact, they found that educational reform, labor reform, and even attempts to create parks and playgrounds became political matters. They learned also that to promote reform in the neighborhood often meant to clash with the ward boss.

Many settlement workers refused to take sides in the political struggle they observed in their neighborhood, and only a small percentage of settlements ever took part in ward politics. Mary Simkhovitch and Robert Woods especially, insisted that the residents had little to gain and much to lose by taking a stand in local politics. "In nearly all cases it is idle for the settlement to attempt to win away the following of local politicians," Woods decided. "To make such an attempt is to leave out of account the loyalties of class, race and religion which bind the people of the crowded wards to their political leaders." Instead of attempting to defeat the ward boss, Woods believed the settlement workers should try to cooperate with him in promoting a program of playgrounds and public baths for the ward. Through a gradual process of education the settlement workers could teach the voters to demand more from their elected representatives and force the ward boss to become an enlightened local leader.

Through co-operation rather than opposition Woods and the other residents at the South End House in Boston were able to accomplish a great deal, but the situation in Boston's ninth ward was not exactly typical. Like most of the downtown wards, the ninth was controlled by the Democratic party, but the political leader in the ward was James Donovan, an affable and reasonable

Irish boss whom Woods called "Honorable Jim." Unlike many local politicians, Donovan seemed to be more concerned with the welfare of the people than with his own pocketbook, and he joined the settlement workers in many projects, including the erection of a public bathhouse. His help was not based entirely on altruism, however. In the fight for political control in Boston, he had lost out to the combined forces of Martin Lomasney and John Fitzgerald. "Honorable Jim" badly needed an ally to protect his position in the ninth ward. By aligning himself with the sedate settlement worker, Donovan was assured of the support of the "better element" in the ward. Woods occasionally supported a candidate for alderman, but never tried to challenge the Democratic party or the political rule of Jim Donovan. In return, Donovan co-operated in the settlement's struggle to improve working and living conditions in the South End. It was a profitable partnership for both the settlement workers and the ward boss.

\*        \*        \*

It was in Chicago that settlement workers played the most significant role in local politics. There, two-party rivalry was part of the political pattern in most wards, making reform campaigns more feasible than in Boston or New York. The presence of an aggressive group of young reformers was equally important in making the settlements a strong influence in Chicago ward politics.

Jane Addams had, typically, little political concern in the beginning; but she came to believe that politics was the most vital interest of the area "and to keep aloof from it must be to lose one opportunity of sharing the life of the neighborhood." A settlement, she decided finally, had no right to get involved in all other parts of community life and ignore politics. In the 1890's the nineteenth ward, where Hull House was located, contained about 50,000 people of twenty different nationalities, all crowded into a few square miles of flimsy, depressing tenement houses. It was a shifting, restless mass of people; the Irish and the Germans still predominated and held much of the political power, but in the last decade of the nineteenth century these two groups were being replaced by Italians, Bohemians, Poles, and Russian Jews. The newer residents had little experience with American customs or American politics, and as one reporter commented, "they are capable of being herded and driven by anyone . . . strong enough to wield the rod."

In the 1890's Johnny Powers did most of the herding and driving in the nineteenth ward. A short, stocky little Irishman with a smooth-shaven face and gray hair, Powers was fifty years old in 1896. He had been the nineteenth ward's alderman since 1888, but he was no ordinary politician—he was one of the most powerful men in Chicago. In 1898 he was chairman of the Finance Committee of the Chicago City Council and boss of the caucus that distributed the chairmanships of the other committees. He controlled the Cook County Democratic Committee, also, and had been personally responsible for giving away millions of dollars in street railway franchises to Charles Yerkes and his associates. In partnership with his political henchman, William J. O'Brien, Powers owned several saloons, one conveniently located near City Hall. Although he drew a salary of three dollars a week for his services as alderman, he lived comfortably in one of the largest houses in the ward and was reportedly worth $400,000 in 1896. "He is coolheaded, cunning and wholly unscrupulous," one reporter decided. "He is the feudal lord who governs his retainers with open-handed liberality or crushes them to poverty as it suits his nearest purpose."

It did not take the Hull House ladies long to realize who controlled the nineteenth ward. They noticed that a large portion of the men in the neighborhood were streetcar employees and many of the girls were telephone operators; it soon became apparent that Johnny Powers was responsible for their employment. And as the settlement workers tried to improve living and working conditions in the ward, they found their plans checkmated at almost every move. Powers acquiesced in the Hull House schemes for a park and a public bath, but when it came to a new public school, he was not so co-operative.

The settlement workers maintained a kindergarten and an elaborate system of clubs and classes that did much to supplement the overcrowded school in the nineteenth ward. They also conducted an investigation that revealed that there were three thousand more pupils in the ward than seats in the school. With these statistics and a petition signed by many residents in the ward, they put their case for a new school before the Chicago School Board. The Board approved, but Powers wanted a new parochial school for the ward. His henchman O'Brien, who was chairman of the City Council Committee on Education, saw to it that the settlement workers' plan was quietly pigeonholed.

Dirty streets disturbed the settlement workers even more than inadequate schools, and the streets of the nineteenth ward were filthy enough to concern anyone who could smell. Slaughterhouses, bakeries, fish peddlers, and livery stables, as well as ordinary citizens, dumped their refuse into streets and alleys that were already clogged with dirt. The Hull House reformers thought at first that a lack of understanding about the spread of disease and a lack of pride in the neighborhood caused the deplorable conditions, so they launched a campaign of education. They held meetings with the mothers in the neighborhood, set up incinerators and boxes, and organized teams to inspect the alleys. It soon became apparent, however, that other factors were responsible for conditions in the nineteenth ward. The workers reported hundreds of violations to the Health Department, but nothing was done about them. They made protests at City Hall, but the filth remained, and the death rate in the nineteenth ward continued to be one of the highest in the city. Jane Addams assigned Edward Burchard to investigate the collection system in the ward, and he discovered that Alderman Powers had used the position of garbage inspector as a political plum, handing it out to a local henchman who was more interested in collecting the money than the garbage.

In the spring of 1895 Jane Addams took direct action to improve the situation. Surprising even her closest friends, she submitted a bid for the collection of garbage in the nineteenth ward. Her bid was finally thrown out on a technicality, but the publicity it received caused the Mayor to appoint her inspector for the nineteenth ward. Miss Addams took her job seriously. She appointed Amanda Johnson, a young graduate of the University of Wisconsin, as her deputy, and together they launched an attack on the filth and the garbage in the ward. They were up at six in the morning to follow the garbage wagons to the dump, and they spent much time keeping charts and maps, complaining to City Hall, arresting landlords, and arguing with the contractor. "The ward is really cleaner," Jane Addams could declare in August 1895, but the campaign against filth convinced the settlement workers that if the ward was to be kept permanently clean, they had to defeat Johnny Powers.

The fight against Powers began with the Hull House Men's Club, which had been organized in 1893. The club met regularly at the settlement and was composed largely of young men from the neighborhood and a few residents. Although they held lectures and discussions on a variety of topics, most of the members were primarily interested in politics. With Jane Addams's encouragement the group nominated one of its members, Frank Lawler, as an independent candidate for alderman in the spring of 1895. Powers was more amused than concerned by the reformers' "Sunday School" attempt to enter ward politics, but with the help of the settlement workers Lawler won. The Hull House victory was short-lived, however, for the successful candidate was unable to resist the attractive inducements put before him by his colleague from the nineteenth ward. Within a matter of months, Frank Lawler, the Hull House reform alderman, was Johnny Powers's most loyal supporter.

Encouraged nevertheless by "victory" in the 1895 campaign, Jane Addams decided to attack Powers himself when he came up for re-election in 1896. In opening the campaign she was thinking beyond the situation in the nineteenth ward. "I really believe," she wrote to Henry Demarest Lloyd, "that if we could get an investigation in the 19th ward against our corporation alderman it might extend to the whole city."

It was not easy to find a candidate willing to oppose Powers, but after a long search the Hull House reformers settled upon William Gleeson, a forty-two-year-old Irish immigrant who was a member of the settlement Men's Club and a former president of the Chicago Bricklayers' Union. Jane Addams persuaded Hazen Pingree, the reform mayor of Detroit, to come to Chicago to open the campaign, despite the fact that Pingree was skeptical about the wisdom of trying to unseat a man like Powers. His feeling was that municipal reform had to start first in the "good" wards, the respectable areas of the city, and then spread gradually to sections like the nineteenth. Jane Addams, however, argued that in Chicago, at least, it was difficult to separate the good wards from the bad, and that, in any case, Powers's influence was city-wide.

As the campaign progressed, the settlement workers attacked

Powers as a tool of the trusts and the street railway magnates. They charged that he had robbed the people of the nineteenth ward by depriving them of clean streets and adequate schools while he amassed a personal fortune. They saturated the ward with posters and placards denouncing, "Yerkes and Powers, the Briber and the Bribed." They bombarded the citizens with handbills listing the grievances suffered by residents of Powers's ward. "Incomparably filthy, ill-paved, and snow-laden streets, high rates, low services, double fares . . . scant public school accommodations, lack of small parks and playgrounds, rapidly increasing tenements . . . taxation that favors the corrupt and oppresses the honest"—these were some of the things that Powers's rule had brought to the nineteenth ward. The reformers promised relief from corruption and advocated municipal ownership of the streetcar lines. Jane Addams used her wide contacts throughout the city to bring outside speakers to the ward. George Cole, chairman of the Committee of One Hundred of the newly organized Municipal Voters' League, spoke to a rally in Hull House gymnasium and assured the crowd that they had the support of the League. Judge Murray F. Tuley addressed a large mass meeting at Central Music Hall and chastised the citizens of the nineteenth ward for not having enough civic pride "to overthrow this prince of the boodlers." The settlement workers, however, received little except sympathy and good wishes from the "better element" in Chicago, and their reform movement went down to defeat. Yet Gleeson did reduce Powers's usual majority. More importantly, the campaign provided the settlement workers with an education in the realities of neighborhood politics.

The Hull House reformers learned, for example, that their crusade for better streets had antagonized the property owners in the ward, since the streets could not be repaved without a special tax assessment. They also learned that it had been unwise to attempt to appeal to the ordinary workingmen in the ward by nominating a workingman to run against Powers. One of the campaign posters showed Gleeson in working clothes eating from a dinner pail while Powers was shown in a dinner jacket drinking champagne. "To the chagrin of the reformers," Jane Addams later noted, ". . . it was gradually discovered that in the popular mind a man who laid bricks and wore overalls was not nearly so desirable for an alderman as the man who drank champagne and wore a diamond in his shirt front. The district wished its representative to stand up to the best of them." By the same token, the rumor that circulated widely during the campaign to the effect that Powers had received the sum of $50,000 from Charles Yerkes for campaign expenses seemed to help Powers more than it hurt him. Yerkes had recently given a large sum to an educational institution, and in the eyes of the average voter in the nineteenth ward he was a good, upright, and philanthropic citizen. In contrast, the professors and reformers who came into the ward from other sections of the city and talked about corruption seemed like cranks to the average voter.

Jane Addams and the other settlement workers also got a lesson in how a successful ward boss operated to win votes. Since Powers considered the Hull House reform movement more of a joke than a threat, he resorted to nothing unusual in 1896. For him, winning votes was a year-round job: he was always on hand. When a death occurred in the neighborhood, Powers provided a stylish burial; he had a standing account at the undertaker's. When a man lost his job, Powers provided him with work; he boasted that 2600 of the residents of the nineteenth ward were on the city's payroll. When a resident of the ward got into trouble, Powers would bail him out of jail and fix matters with the judge. If a citizen of the ward needed to travel out of the city, Powers got him a free pass on the railroad. At Christmas time the loyal voter could expect a turkey from the benevolent alderman, and when Powers made gifts it was with none of the restrictions of the charity organization society. Soon after the election of 1896, the reformers discovered that many of the people in the ward who had supported the Hull House candidate expected the settlement to continue to act like a ward boss. The settlement workers were besieged with requests for aid, for help in bailing a son out of jail or getting a husband a job. Hull House could challenge Johnny Powers at election time, but the settlement could not begin to compete with the benevolent ward boss when it came to passing out favors.

Despite attempts by the settlement workers to attack Powers as a corrupt man who robbed the city treasury, took bribes from the street railway magnates, and lined his own coffers while giving the nineteenth ward little in return, they could not change the image in the mind of the average voter—the image of Powers as a good friend and neighbor, who could be depended on in time of trouble. Even before the election, Jane Addams hit upon the secret of Johnny Powers's success as a ward politician. "He isn't elected because he is dishonest," she decided. "He is elected because he is a friendly visitor."

Only after the campaign of 1896, however, did she begin to realize how persuasive and skillful Powers was. In the two years following the election, Powers offered a job to nearly every man who had been prominent in the campaign against him. Most of these men were members of the Hull House Men's Club. He appointed a printer who had played an important role in the reform campaign to a clerkship at City Hall. He gave a driver a new job and a large salary at the police barns, and offered William Gleeson, his opposing candidate, a lucrative position in the city construction department.

Jane Addams and the other settlement workers were still not convinced that Powers was unbeatable. They pondered their mistakes, added up the lessons they had learned, and vowed they would defeat Powers in 1898. They were encouraged by the large vote piled up in 1897 by John Maynard Harlan, a reform candidate for mayor, and pleased by the passage of a new civil service law and by the election of a reform alderman in the seventeenth ward. Reform seemed to be in the air in Chicago in the last years of the nineteenth century, and reform was surely needed in the nineteenth ward.

Powers himself provided fresh incentive for the reform movement in 1898. Although he continued to give away streetcar franchises and was constantly in the news because of illegal gambling in his saloons, his attack on the settlement worker who was deputy garbage inspector aroused anew the wrath of the Hull House residents. In 1896, when the position of garbage inspector became a civil service job, Amanda Johnson took the examination and passed at the top of the list. It looked as though Powers had permanently lost a job for one of his heelers. Early in January 1898, however, he demanded that the Civil Service Commission discharge Miss Johnson from her post because she had been actively campaigning against him and finding fault with his record as alderman. The

newspapers as well as the Commission found Miss Johnson innocent, but Powers, as chairman of the Finance Committee of the
City Council, decided that it was necessary to cut expenses. By
merging the Bureau of Street and Alley Cleaning with the Department of Streets, he deprived Miss Johnson of her job.

Over four hundred people meeting in Hull House gymnasium
"sizzled and boiled" with indignation over Powers's attack on Miss
Johnson; one of the speakers called him a disgrace to Ireland and
the Catholic religion. A few days later the reformers held another
meeting at Hull House and elected Professor William Hill of the
University of Chicago chairman of a campaign committee that prepared once again to do battle with Johnny Powers. Hill had earlier
moved to Hull House in order to vote in the ward.

Jane Addams officially opened the campaign against Powers with
a remarkable address to the Chicago Ethical Culture Society on
Sunday, January 23, 1898. The speech, which received nation-wide
publicity, was at once an attack on Johnny Powers and his methods
(although his name was never mentioned) and a shrewd analysis
of the forces and motives involved in city politics at the ward level.
It was one of the first attempts to analyze the methods and motives
of a city boss. "There has been no more important contribution to
the literature of municipal government, and the study of its problems . . . ," John Gavit, editor of the *Commons* decided, and Robert
Woods wrote Miss Addams, "I think it is the best thing you have
ever done with the pen."

Miss Addams based her address on the experience of two campaigns and eight years of observation in the nineteenth ward. "The
successful candidate must be a good man according to the standards of his constituents," she emphasized. "He must not attempt
to hold up a morality beyond them, nor must he attempt to reform
or change the standard. His safety lies in doing, on a large scale,
the good deeds which his constituents are able to do only on a small
scale." She gave concrete illustrations from her experience of how
a boss was able to remain in power, and she blamed the reformers
for not learning from the boss. When compared with a colorful figure
like Johnny Powers, most reformers seemed drab indeed. "The reformers give themselves over largely to criticism of the present state
of affairs, to writing and talking of what the future must be," she

decided, "but their goodness is not dramatic; it is not even concrete and human."

Even though Jane Addams could understand why a man like Powers was re-elected time after time, she did not condone his actions. She attacked him for assigning city jobs in violation of the civil service law, and for saving men from prison and "fixing things" with the judge. His actions had a "blighting effect on public morals," she charged. "The positive evils of corrupt government are bound to fall heaviest upon the poorest and least capable," she decided. Powers gave away street railway franchises, and the people in the nineteenth ward had to pay an increased fare. He gave them turkeys at Christmas time, but he refused to give them clean streets and more public schools.

Powers meanwhile had grown annoyed with the publicity he was getting because of the settlement workers. "The trouble with Miss Addams," he told a reporter, "is that she is just jealous of my charitable work in the ward." But he was in no mood to risk defeat in 1898; there was too much money at stake. Charles Yerkes was planning to ask the Council for an ordinance extending the street railway franchise for fifty years. By making sure the Council cooperated, Powers stood to share the gain, but he first had to be re-elected, and Jane Addams was all that stood in his way. "Hull House will be driven from the ward, and its leaders will be forced to shut up shop," Powers angrily predicted as he opened his attack on the settlement workers.

Powers was not the only one to criticize Jane Addams and Hull House. The *Chicago Chronicle,* a newspaper with a vested interest in the street railway franchises, issued attack after attack on the reformers. Some of the Catholic priests in the nineteenth ward, out of jealousy and because their churches received a large amount of money from Powers, campaigned actively against Hull House, charging that the settlement was anti-Catholic and anti-immigrant. Posters and placards appeared denouncing "petticoat government," and Jane Addams received letters—some of them obscene—praising "that good, noble, and charitable man, Johnny Powers," and pointing out that by living in the slums and entering politics she had "long since forgot the pride and dignity so much admired in a beautiful woman. . . ."

The settlement workers fought back. They finally found an appealing candidate who would not sell out to Powers—Simeon Armstrong. Armstrong had lived in the ward for thirty years, and was, like Powers, Irish and Catholic and a member of the Democratic party. The reformers persuaded the Republican organization in the ward to nominate Armstrong so that the opposition to Powers would be concentrated on one candidate. The Hull House Men's Club, which had been reorganized after the election of 1896, formed a Nineteenth Ward Improvement Committee which established an organization in every precinct in the ward.

The Hull House reformers printed and distributed posters, made speeches, followed up rumors of fraud, and helped to co-ordinate the precinct organizations, but they were forced to devote much of their time to raising money. Florence Kelley, Ellen Gates Starr, and Alzina Stevens worked hard in the campaign, and George Hooker, director of the Chicago City Club, supplied the campaign speakers with statistics proving Powers's corruption. Mary Kenny O'Sullivan came back to Hull House from Boston for the campaign. Well known in the nineteenth ward, she proved a valuable aid in quieting some of the Catholic opposition. One of the Italian newspapers in Chicago, *La Tribuna Italiana,* opposed Powers, and John Harlan, "the tiger of the twenty-second ward," came into the nineteenth to answer some of Powers's charges against Hull House. "There are signs that the nineteenth ward is beginning to get ashamed of Powers," he announced to a packed auditorium. "The Women of Hull House have headed the revolt against him. They have no votes, but they have influence. They have helped more people than Powers, and those whom they have aided know that it has not been done for selfish motives."

Despite flowery speeches, outside support, and a vigorous campaign, the Hull House reformers were defeated again. The final results were: Powers, 5450; Armstrong, 2249. Powers had not only won; he had also wiped out the gains the reformers had made two years previously and restored his usual margin of victory.

Ray Stannard Baker, the muckraking journalist who spent a few weeks at Hull House during the campaign, saw indications that Powers would be re-elected even before the results were in. Some of the small businessmen who had supported Armstrong early in the campaign began to drop away. Powers dropped a hint to a landlord here or a coal dealer there, and the men decided that they could not afford to rebel. A threat or rumor that a peddler would lose his license or a city employee his job was enough to prevent many from supporting Hull House and Simeon Armstrong. The settlement workers made elaborate efforts to limit the number of frauds in the registration and voting, but as Jane Addams remarked on the day before the election, with nearly everybody corrupt, it was "hard to prove anything."

In gloating over his victory, Johnny Powers paraphrased the words Jane Addams had used at the beginning of the campaign. "I may not be the sort of man the reformers like," he announced, "but I am what my people like, and neither Hull House nor all the reformers in town can turn them against me." Yet shortly after the election, a measure to enlarge one of the public schools in the ward was approved by the Board of Education and passed by City Council. Johnny Powers and the Catholic priests, who had opposed such an enlargement for seven years, were strangely silent. Perhaps the settlement workers' efforts had not been entirely in vain.

After the campaign excitement died, the inevitable question had to be answered—should the settlement workers continue to oppose the ward boss? Florence Kelley, one of the most able of the group, believed that the fight should be continued. To admit defeat, to withdraw from politics, she argued, would be to accept the conventional ethics of too many organizations that preached reform in theory but failed to practise it in fact. "True to its avowed purpose 'to provide a centre for a higher civic and social life,' Hull House entered the campaigns of 1896 and 1898 to make its protest on behalf of municipal honesty," Florence Kelley maintained, "and from that task it cannot turn back."

Jane Addams could not agree. She had no intention of revising the original purpose of Hull House, but she was more pragmatic than Mrs. Kelley and believed that little more could be accomplished by trying again to defeat Powers. She had learned a great deal about the realities of ward politics and more about the limitations of reform movements. She had also learned that it was impossible to accomplish much in one ward, that it was necessary to move to the city and beyond.

Only a short distance from Hull House, in the seventeenth ward, Chicago Commons continued to play an important role in ward politics long after Jane Addams had given up the task of unseating Powers. The seventeenth ward was as crowded and as dirty as the nineteenth, but with one major difference; the seventeenth ward did not have a Johnny Powers. There were political bosses, of course, but one man had never been able to consolidate his control and build an empire in the seventeenth ward as Powers had done. The absence of one powerful boss and the presence of an aggressive group of young reformers allowed Chicago Commons to build a ward organization that controlled the political balance of power for nearly two decades.

\*     \*     \*

The settlement workers' impact on local politics in the seventeenth ward in Chicago was impressive and unusual, but whether they were participants in local politics or merely observers, and regardless of whether they defeated the ward boss or were defeated by him, the settlement workers invariably came to appreciate the usefulness of the politician and to learn from him, even as they despaired his lack of honesty and civic pride. They were among the first to analyze the source of the bosses' strength. But they also learned that little could be accomplished in a single ward, and they were led to participate in a variety of city-wide reform campaigns.

# IV BUSINESSMEN, SOCIALISTS, AND MUNICIPAL REFORM

Samuel P. Hays

# BUSINESS ELITE AND THE CENTRALIZATION OF DECISION-MAKING

*Lincoln Steffens saw urban Progressive reform as an uprising of a public demanding "good government" against the political machines and their allied business interests; Samuel P. Hays contends that reform in municipal government during the Progressive era was often business inspired. In Pittsburgh, for example, a new business elite, coming to power with the growth of industry during the last part of the nineteenth century, stimulated municipal reform. With interests that encompassed an entire range of city-wide activities, these businessmen reformers worked to centralize decision-making and to remove power from the wards and neighborhoods, represented by the boss and his machine. Although Steffens and other Progressives saw reform, such as the city commission and manager forms of government and city-wide school boards and election of councilmen, as increasing popular participation in government, Hays contends they actually reduced it. By employing empirical data, Hays attempts to separate the ideology and rhetoric of Progressive reform from its practice. He is author of* The Response to Industrialism *and* Conservation and the Gospel of Efficiency *as well as several articles on new approaches to American history.*

In order to achieve a more complete understanding of social change in the Progressive Era, historians must now undertake a deeper analysis of the practices of economic, political, and social groups. Political ideology alone is no longer satisfactory evidence to describe social patterns because generalizations based upon it, which tend to divide political groups into the moral and the immoral, the rational and the irrational, the efficient and the inefficient, do not square with political practice. Behind this contemporary rhetoric concerning the nature of reform lay patterns of political behavior which were at variance with it. Since an extensive gap separated ideology and practice, we can no longer take the former as an accurate description of the latter, but must reconstruct social behavior from other types of evidence.

Reform in urban government provides one of the most striking

Reprinted by permission of the *Pacific Northwest Quarterly* and the author from Samuel P. Hays, "The Politics of Reform in Municipal Government in the Progressive Era," *Pacific Northwest Quarterly*, 55 (October 1964), pp. 157–169.

examples of this problem of analysis. The demand for change in municipal affairs, whether in terms of over-all reform, such as the commission and city-manager plans, or of more piecemeal modifications, such as the development of city-wide school boards, deeply involved reform ideology. Reformers loudly proclaimed a new structure of municipal government as more moral, more rational, and more efficient and, because it was so, self-evidently more desirable. But precisely because of this emphasis, there seemed to be no need to analyze the political forces behind change. Because the goals of reform were good, its causes were obvious; rather than being the product of particular people and particular ideas in particular situations, they were deeply imbedded in the universal impulses and truths of "progress." Consequently, historians have rarely tried to determine precisely who the municipal reformers were or what they did, but instead have relied on reform ideology as an accurate description of reform practice.

The reform ideology which became the basis of historical analysis is well known. It appears in classic form in Lincoln Steffens' *Shame of the Cities.* The urban political struggle of the Progressive Era, so the argument goes, involved a conflict between public impulses for "good government" against a corrupt alliance of "machine politicians" and "special interests."

During the rapid urbanization of the late 19th century, the latter had been free to aggrandize themselves, especially through franchise grants, at the expense of the public. Their power lay primarily in their ability to manipulate the political process, by bribery and corruption, for their own ends. Against such arrangements there gradually arose a public protest, a demand by the public for honest government, for officials who would act for the public rather than for themselves. To accomplish their goals, reformers sought basic modifications in the political system, both in the structure of government and in the manner of selecting public officials. These changes, successful in city after city, enabled the "public interest" to triumph.

Recently, George Mowry, Alfred Chandler, Jr., and Richard Hofstadter have modified this analysis by emphasizing the fact that the impulse for reform did not come from the working class. This might have been suspected from the rather strained efforts of National Municipal League writers in the "Era of Reform" to go out of their way to demonstrate working-class support for commission and city-manager governments. We now know that they clutched at straws, and often erroneously, in order to prove to themselves as well as to the public that municipal reform was a mass movement.

The Mowry-Chandler-Hofstadter writings have further modified older views by asserting that reform in general and municipal reform in particular sprang from a distinctively middle-class movement. This has now become the prevailing view. Its popularity is surprising not only because it is based upon faulty logic and extremely limited evidence, but also because it, too, emphasizes the analysis of ideology rather than practice and fails to contribute much to the understanding of who distinctively were involved in reform and why.

Ostensibly, the "middle-class" theory of reform is based upon a new type of behavioral evidence, the collective biography, in studies by Mowry of California Progressive party leaders, by Chandler of a nationwide group of that party's leading figures, and by Hofstadter of four professions—ministers, lawyers, teachers, editors. These studies demonstrate the middle-class nature of reform, but they fail to determine if reformers were distinctively middle class, specifically if they differed from their opponents. One study of 300 political leaders in the state of Iowa, for example, discovered that Progressive party, Old Guard, and Cummins Republicans were all substantially alike, the Progressives differing only in that they were slightly younger than the others and had less political experience. If its opponents were also middle class, then one cannot describe Progressive reform as a phenomenon, the special nature of which can be explained in terms of middle-class characteristics. One cannot explain the distinctive behavior of people in terms of characteristics which are not distinctive to them.

\*        \*        \*

The weakness of the "middle-class" theory of reform stems from the fact that it rests primarily upon ideological evidence, not on a thorough-going description of political practice. Although the studies of Mowry, Chandler, and Hofstadter ostensibly derive from behavioral evidence, they actually derive largely from the extensive expressions of middle-ground ideological position, of the reformers' own descriptions of their contemporary society, and of their expressed fears of both the lower and the upper classes, of the fright of being ground between the millstones of labor and capital.

Such evidence, though it accurately portrays what people thought, does not accurately describe what they did. The great majority of Americans look upon themselves as "middle class" and subscribe to a middle-ground ideology, even though in practice they belong to a great variety of distinct social classes. Such ideologies are not rationalizations or deliberate attempts to deceive. They are natural phenomena of human behavior. But the historian should be especially sensitive to their role so that he will not take evidence of political ideology as an accurate representation of political practice.

In the following account I will summarize evidence in both secondary and primary works concerning the political practices in which municipal reformers were involved. Such an analysis logically can be broken down into three parts, each one corresponding to a step in the traditional argument. First, what was the source of reform? Did it lie in the general public rather than in particular groups? Was it middle class, working class, or perhaps of other composition? Second, what was the reform target of attack? Were reformers primarily interested in ousting the corrupt individual, the political or business leader who made private arrangements at the expense of the public, or were they interested in something else? Third, what political innovations did reformers bring about? Did they seek to expand popular participation in the governmental process?

There is now sufficient evidence to determine the validity of these specific elements of the more general argument. Some of it has been available for several decades; some has appeared more recently; some is presented here for the first time. All of it adds up to the conclusion that reform in municipal government involved a political development far different from what we have assumed in the past.

Available evidence indicates that the source of support for reform in municipal government did not come from the lower or middle classes, but from the upper class. The leading business groups in

each city and professional men closely allied with them initiated and
dominated municipal movements. . . .

*      *      *

The character of municipal reform is demonstrated more precisely by a brief examination of the movements in Des Moines and
Pittsburgh. The Des Moines Commerical Club inaugurated and carefully controlled the drive for the commission form of government.
In January, 1906, the Club held a so-called "mass meeting" of business and professional men to secure an enabling act from the state
legislature. P. C. Kenyon, president of the Club, selected a Committee of 300, composed principally of business and professional
men, to draw up a specific proposal. After the legislature approved
their plan, the same committee managed the campaign which persuaded the electorate to accept the commission form of government
by a narrow margin in June, 1907.

In this election the lower-income wards of the city opposed the
change, the upper-income wards supported it strongly, and the
middle-income wards were more evenly divided. In order to control
the new government, the Committee of 300, now expanded to 530,
sought to determine the nomination and election of the five new
commissioners, and to this end they selected an avowedly businessman's slate. Their plans backfired when the voters swept into office
a slate of anticommission candidates who now controlled the new
commission government.

Proponents of the commission form of government in Des Moines
spoke frequently in the name of the "people." But their more
explicit statements emphasized their intent that the new plan be a
"business system" of government, run by businessmen. The slate
of candidates for commissioner endorsed by advocates of the plan
was known as the "businessman's ticket." J. W. Hill, president of
the committees of 300 and 530, bluntly declared: "The professional
politician must be ousted and in his place capable business men
chosen to conduct the affairs of the city." I. M. Earle, general
counsel of the Bankers Life Association and a prominent figure in
the movement, put the point more precisely: "When the plan was
adopted it was the intention to get businessmen to run it."

Although reformers used the ideology of popular government, they in no sense meant that all segments of society should be involved equally in municipal decision-making. They meant that their concept of the city's welfare would be best achieved if the business community controlled city government. As one businessman told a labor audience, the businessman's slate represented labor "better than you do yourself."

The composition of the municipal reform movement in Pittsburgh demonstrates its upper-class and professional as well as its business sources. Here the two principal reform organizations were the Civic Club and the Voters' League. The 745 members of these two organizations came primarily from the upper class. Sixty-five per cent appeared in upper-class directories which contained the names of only 2 percent of the city's families. Furthermore, many who were not listed in these directories lived in upper-class areas. These reformers, it should be stressed, comprised not an old but a new upper class. Few came from earlier industrial and mercantile families. Most of them had risen to social position from wealth created after 1870 in the iron, steel, electrical equipment, and other industries, and they lived in the newer rather than the older fashionable areas.

Almost half (48 per cent) of the reformers were professional men: doctors, lawyers, ministers, directors of libraries and museums, engineers, architects, private and public school teachers, and college professors. Some of these belonged to the upper class as well, especially the lawyers, ministers, and private school teachers. But for the most part their interest in reform stemmed from the inherent dynamics of their professions rather than from their class connections. They came from the more advanced segments of their organizations, from those in the forefront of the acquisition and application of knowledge. They were not the older professional men, seeking to preserve the past against change; they were in the vanguard of professional life, actively seeking to apply expertise more widely to public affairs.

Pittsburgh reformers included a large segment of businessmen; 52 per cent were bankers and corporation officials or their wives. Among them were the presidents of fourteen large banks and officials of Westinghouse, Pittsburgh Plate Glass, U.S. Steel and its component parts (such as Carnegie Steel, American Bridge, and

National Tube), Jones and Laughlin, lesser steel companies (such as Crucible, Pittsburgh, Superior, Lockhart, and H. K. Porter), the H. J. Heinz Company, and the Pittsburgh Coal Company, as well as officials of the Pennsylvania Railroad and the Pittsburgh and Lake Erie. These men were not small businessmen; they directed the most powerful banking and industrial organizations of the city. They represented not the old business community, but industries which had developed and grown primarily within the past fifty years and which had come to dominate the city's economic life.

These business, professional, and upper-class groups who dominated municipal reform movements were all involved in the rationalization and systematization of modern life; they wished a form of government which would be more consistent with the objectives inherent in those developments. The most important single feature of their perspective was the rapid expansion of the geographical scope of affairs which they wished to influence and manipulate, a scope which was no longer limited and narrow, no longer within the confines of pedestrian communities, but was now broad and city-wide, covering the whole range of activities of the metropolitan area.

The migration of the upper class from central to outlying areas created a geographical distance between its residential communities and its economic institutions. To protect the latter required involvement both in local ward affairs and in the larger city government as well. Moreover, upper-class cultural institutions, such as museums, libraries, and symphony orchestras, required an active interest in the larger muncipal context from which these institutions drew much of their clientele.

Professional groups, broadening the scope of affairs which they sought to study, measure, or manipulate, also sought to influence the public health, the educational system, or the physical arrangements of the entire city. Their concerns were limitless, not bounded by geography, but as expansive as the professional imagination. Finally, the new industrial community greatly broadened its perspective in governmental affairs because of its new recognition of the way in which factors throughout the city affected business growth. The increasing size and scope of industry, the greater stake in more varied and geographically dispersed facets of city life, the effect of floods on many business concerns, the need to promote traffic flows to and from work for both blue-collar and managerial employees—all contributed to this larger interest. The geographically larger private perspectives of upper-class, professional, and business groups gave rise to a geographically larger public perspective.

These reformers were dissatisfied with existing systems of municipal government. They did not oppose corruption per se—although there was plenty of that. They objected to the structure of government which enabled local and particularistic interests to dominate. Prior to the reforms of the Progressive Era, city government consisted primarily of confederations of local wards, each of which was represented on the city's legislative body. Each ward frequently had its own elementary schools and ward-elected school boards which administered them.

These particularistic interests were the focus of a decentralized political life. City councilmen were local leaders. They spoke for their local areas, the economic interests of their inhabitants, their residential concerns, their educational, recreational, and religious interests—i.e., for those aspects of community life which mattered most to those they represented. They rolled logs in the city council to provide streets, sewers, and other public works for their local areas. They defended the community's cultural practices, its distinctive languages or national customs, its liberal attitude toward liquor, and its saloons and dance halls which served as centers of community life. . . . In short, pre-reform officials spoke for their constituencies, inevitably their own wards which had elected them, rather than for other sections or groups of the city.

The ward system of government especially gave representation in city affairs to lower- and middle-class groups. Most elected ward officials were from these groups, and they, in turn, constituted the major opposition to reforms in municipal government. In Pittsburgh, for example, immediately prior to the changes in both the city council and the school board in 1911 in which city-wide representation replaced ward representation, only 24 per cent of the 387 members of those bodies represented the same managerial, professional, and banker occupations which dominated the membership of the Civic Club and the Voters' League. The great majority (67 per cent) were

small businessmen—grocers, saloonkeepers, livery-stable propri-
etors, owners of small hotels, druggists—white-collar workers such
as clerks and bookkeepers, and skilled and unskilled workmen.

This decentralized system of urban growth and the institutions
which arose from it reformers now opposed. Social, professional,
and economic life had developed not only in the local wards in a
small community context, but also on a larger scale had become
highly integrated and organized, giving rise to a superstructure of
social organization which lay far above that of ward life and which
was sharply divorced from it in both personal contacts and perspective.

By the late 19th century, those involved in these larger institutions found that the decentralized system of political life limited
their larger objectives. The movement for reform in municipal government, therefore, constituted an attempt by upper-class, advanced
professional, and large business groups to take formal political
power from the previously dominant lower- and middle-class elements so that they might advance their own conceptions of desirable public policy. These two groups came from entirely different
urban worlds, and the political system fashioned by one was no
longer acceptable to the other.

Lower- and middle-class groups not only dominated the pre-reform governments, but vigorously opposed reform. It is significant
that none of the occupational groups among them, for example,
small businessmen or white-collar workers, skilled or unskilled
artisans, had important representation in reform organizations thus
far examined.

\*　　\*　　\*

The most visible opposition to reform and the most readily available target of reform attack was the so-called "machine," for
through the "machine" many different ward communities as well as
lower- and middle-income groups joined effectively to influence the
central city government. Their private occupational and social life
did not naturally involve these groups in larger city-wide activities
in the same way as the upper class was involved; hence they lacked
access to privately organized economic and social power on which

they could construct political power. The "machine" filled this organizational gap.

Yet it should never be forgotten that the social and economic institutions in the wards themselves provided the "machine's" sustaining support and gave it larger significance. When reformers attacked the "machine" as the most visible institutional element of the ward system, they attacked the entire ward form of political organization, and the political power of lower- and middle-income groups which lay behind it.

Reformers often gave the impression that they opposed merely the corrupt politician and his "machine." But in a more fundamental way they looked upon the deficiencies of pre-reform political leaders in terms not of their personal shortcomings, but of the limitations inherent in their occupational, institutional, and class positions. In 1911 the Voters' League of Pittsburgh wrote in its pamphlet analyzing the qualifications of candidates that "a man's occupation ought to give a strong indication of his qualifications for membership on a school board." Certain occupations inherently disqualified a man from serving:

> *Employment as ordinary laborer and in the lowest class of mill work would naturally lead to the conclusion that such men did not have sufficient education or business training to act as school directors. . . . Objection might also be made to small shopkeepers, clerks, workmen at many trades, who by lack of educational advantages and business training, could not, no matter how honest, be expected to administer properly the affairs of an educational system, requiring special knowledge, and where millions are spent each year.*

These, of course, were precisely the groups which did dominate Pittsburgh government prior to reform. The League deplored the fact that school boards contained only a small number of "men prominent throughout the city in business life . . . in professional occupations . . . holding positions as managers, secretaries, auditors, superintendents and foremen" and exhorted these classes to participate more actively as candidates for office.

Reformers, therefore, wished not simply to replace bad men with good; they proposed to change the occupational and class origins of decision-makers. Toward this end they sought innovations in the formal machinery of government which would concentrate political power by sharply centralizing the processes of decision-making rather than distribute it through more popular participation in public affairs. According to the liberal view of the Progressive Era, the major political innovations of reform involved the equalization of political power through the primary, the direct election of public officials, and the initiative, referendum, and recall. These measures played a large role in the political ideology of the time and were frequently incorporated into new municipal charters. But they provided at best only an occasional and often incidental process of decision-making. Far more important in continuous, sustained, day-to-day processes of government were those innovations which centralized decision-making in the hands of fewer and fewer people.

*James Weinstein*

# BUSINESSMEN AND THE CITY COMMISSION AND MANAGER MOVEMENTS

*Like Hays, James Weinstein finds businessmen during the Progressive era supporting such structural urban reforms as the city commission and manager forms of government. Attempting to rationalize and systematize urban life, the businessmen were prime movers for such change, while municipal Socialists often opposed the manager and commission systems. The Socialists saw this centralization of decision-making as weakening their grassroots ward and neighborhood strength. Yet, when businessmen advocated planning and sometimes even municipal ownership for efficiency, the Socialists often found themselves in agreement. This concomitance of business and Socialist interests should lead the student to reflect upon the meaning of municipal Socialism in American urban life. James Weinstein is former editor of* Studies on the Left *and the author of several books and articles dealing with twentieth-century American history.*

On a national scale big businessmen tended to be the leaders for reform and regulation, while the smaller manufacturers and com-

From James Weinstein, *The Corporate Ideal in the Liberal State: 1900–1918,* Chapter 4. Copyright © 1968 by James Weinstein. Reprinted by permission of Beacon Press.

mercial men often took a narrower, or more immediately interest-conscious, view. In the movement for an interstate trade commission, later embodied in the Federal Trade Commission, and in the agitation for workmen's compensation . . . the executives of leading financial institutions and of large corporations (especially those associated with the National Civic Federation), assumed the initiative. The National Association of Manufacturers, which represented small manufacturers and was suspicious of financiers, dragged its feet until its membership was gradually converted to support for, or acquiescence in, the new reforms. But on a municipal level the small businessman sometimes displayed a broader vision. He was in his own domain and tended, on this scale, to assume attitudes of social responsibility. As participants in local chambers of commerce and boards of trade, local businessmen could identify the future of their cities with that of their own business interests. To rationalize and make more attractive a particular city meant more business for its local entrepreneurs. The centralization of power, or the removal of decision making from "politics," favored businessmen over workingmen or white collar employees. In no area of political or social reform did small businessmen more clearly demonstrate the force of this logic than in the movements for city commission and manager governments.

The idea later embodied in commission and council manager government was enunciated as early as 1896 by Dayton, Ohio, industrial pioneer, John H. Patterson. In a speech at the Dayton centennial, the founder and president of the National Cash Register Company argued that "a city is a great business enterprise whose stockholders are the people." If Patterson had his way, "municipal affairs would be placed on a strict business basis" and directed "not by partisans, either Republican or Democratic, but by men who are skilled in business management and social science." It was not until five years after Patterson spoke that the first commission government came into being, and it was a dozen years before the movement took root and began rapidly to spread. At first, the commission idea was only one plan in what a leading civic reformer described in 1903 as a "hopeless diversity" of remedies for the inefficiency and poor service of American city governments. Yet so well did this "most far reaching progressive proposal for institutional change" fulfill the requirements of business that it was quickly adopted by hundreds of boards of trade and chambers of commerce. Today commission and council manager governments are the prevailing forms of municipal organization, in use in almost half of all American cities. *← of what size ?*

Of course, the drive for municipal reform at the turn of the century did not come from businessmen alone. Graft, corruption, and the misery of slum life had been given wide publicity by reformers and journalists, and by single taxers and socialists. Muckrakers Jacob Riis, Lincoln Steffens, B. O. Flower, and others had exposed the "Shame of the Cities"; successful reform movements had been led by mayors Tom Johnson of Cleveland and Samuel (Golden Rule) Jones of Toledo, and by many other men less well known. The business community did not support this variety of reform, tinged as it was with radical social theories. Indeed, many early reformers concluded that business interests strongly supported the old system of corruption. In 1906 the Cleveland reformer, Frederick C. Howe, wrote that it was "privilege of an industrial rather than a personal sort that has given birth to the boss." Howe had entered political life "with the conviction that our evils were traceable to personal causes"—to the "foreign voter" and to the indifference of the "best" citizens. But experience forced him to a new belief: democracy had failed "by virtue of the privileged interests which have taken possession of our institutions for their own enrichment." From a belief in a "businessman's government" he, like Lincoln Steffens and journalist-reformer Brand Whitlock, had come to believe in a "people's government." Even so conservative a man as William J. Gaynor, mayor of New York City, commented in 1910 that the true corrupters were the "so-called 'leading' citizens" who "get a million dollars out of the city dishonestly while the 'boss' gets a thousand." *businessmen as structural reformers*

As Howe understood, businessmen opposed social reformers such as Jones and Johnson because their administrations disrupted the working relationships between business and the local political machine without providing a suitable and dependable alternative—and also because Jones and Johnson increased the political power of labor and radicals. Aversion to graft, alone, was not enough to move businessmen to sponsor reform. Though costly, business had accepted and lived with graft for many years. [What converted these men into civic reformers was the increased importance of the public functions of the twentieth-century city.] Streets had to be paved for newly developed motor vehicles; harbors had to be deepened and wharves improved for big, new freighters. In addition, electric lighting systems, street railways, sewage disposal plants, water supplies, and fire departments had to be installed or drastically improved to meet the needs of inhabitants, human and commercial, of hundreds of rapidly growing industrial centers.

Municipal services had always been expensive, but as they increased in magnitude and number, costs tended to grow more and more burdensome. In city after city, business circles came to realize that something had to be done. Boston in 1909 was described as "another city whose businessmen have awakened to a new sense of their civic responsibilities" because "the debt of the city was increasing by leaps and bounds, apparently out of all proportion to the improvements for which it was incurred." At the same time the "extraordinary expenses" of municipal services in Chicago moved the Commercial Club of that city to work out a "general scheme of public improvements," known as the "Plan of Chicago." [In the search for alternatives, the commission and manager plans emerged as most promising. They offered stability; they were less expensive; they were devoid of commitment to radical social theories; and they assured businessmen of a more direct and central role in municipal affairs.]

The first commission government emerged from the backwash of the great tidal wave that virtually destroyed Galveston, Texas, in 1900. Left in ruins, with a government unable to cope with the situation, the city was on the edge of bankruptcy. In the emergency, the old, corrupt aldermanic system was abandoned and an organization of local businessmen, the Deepwater Committee, took control. This group, which had been formed earlier to promote harbor improvements, looked on Galveston "not as a city, but [as] a great ruined business." Setting out to establish a new government capable of quick, efficient action in rebuilding a modern city and port, these businessmen evolved a plan for government that closely followed the most efficient form of organization known to them: the business corporation. The theory of the commission plan echoed John H. Patterson's view. It was that "a municipality is largely a business corporation," and, as such, that it should seek "to apply business methods to public service." The voters were seen as stockholders, and the commissioners as corresponding to the board of directors of "an ordinary business corporation."

As adopted, the Galveston plan provided for a five man commission vested with the combined powers of mayor and board of aldermen. Each commissioner headed a city department and functioned as legislator and administrator. The Commission, because it handled all city business, could act promptly and efficiently, and the relative prominence and broad powers given each commissioner "assured" the attraction of "good" men to office. In short, it was a plan to make government more businesslike and to attract businessmen to government.

Commission government spread rapidly through Texas: first to Houston in 1903, then by 1907 to Dallas, Dennison, Fort Worth, El Paso, Greenville, and Sherman. In 1907 Des Moines, Iowa, enacted a commission charter, and to the accompaniment of nationwide publicity the "Texas Idea" was renamed for its Northern imitator. By 1913 over 300 cities from coast to coast had adopted the "Des Moines Plan."

Yet even while commission government was winning quick and widespread acceptance, serious structural weaknesses appeared. The election of popular but incompetent administrators, men who played politics better than they ran city departments, revealed the disadvantages of combining executive and legislative functions in the commissioners. Individual commissioners often attempted to consolidate their positions by securing excessive appropriations in order either to strengthen their own departments or simply to reward their supporters with city jobs. Since the commissions as a whole fixed both appropriations and policy, the consent of the other commissioners was necessary, and a system of favor-trading often developed in the commissions, side by side with interdepartmental rivalries. In many cases "five separate governments" tended to develop around the five commissioners.

To overcome these weaknesses, municipal reform leader H. S. Gilbertson drew up a "commission-manager" plan in 1910, and the board of trade of Lockport, New York, sponsored it as its proposed new city charter. The Lockport proposal, as Gilbertson's plan was called, separated the legislative and executive functions by retaining an elected commission to legislate for the city, while providing for an appointed manager to assume all executive functions. Under this plan executive ability was no longer a prerequisite for successful commissioners. At the same time the day-to-day management of city affairs was removed from more direct political pressures by the creation of an independent office for the manager, who was hired on a contractual basis to carry out the policies set by the commission.

Under the Lockport proposal departmental appointments, as well as the expenditure of city funds, were, for the most part, placed in the manager's hands. Despite the efforts of the Lockport board of trade, the manager charter was defeated in the New York legislature in 1911, and once again the South took the lead when Sumter, South Carolina, secured a "commission-manager" charter the same year. But, as with the original commission plan, the manager movement received national impetus only after a Northern city, Dayton, Ohio, adopted the plan in 1913. Thereafter, the "Dayton Plan" spread rapidly, and in six years more than 130 cities had put through manager charters.

The initiative for commission and manager government came consistently from chambers of commerce and other organized business groups; they were the decisive element, in coalition with civic reformers, which made the movement a sweeping success.

*       *       *

The manager movement, like the commission, also was led by chambers of commerce and boards of trade. The first manager charter in Sumter, South Carolina, for example, was promoted by the local chamber. Dayton was a model of business sponsorship. There the chamber of commerce set up a committee of five members, headed by John H. Patterson. He set up a Bureau of Municipal Research, which, in turn, "plunged into an aggressive campaign of public education."

Meanwhile, the chamber "began to suspect that its open sponsorship of a new charter might seem an evil omen to many of the ordinary workingclass voters." Accordingly, it ceased its official participation, and the original committee was increased, first to fifteen, and finally to one hundred. The new citizens' committee then hired the former secretary of the Detroit Board of Commerce, who built a broad coalition in support of the reform. Despite these efforts the opposition to the new charter on the part of the Democratic and Socialist parties appeared to doom the manager plan in Dayton, until, as in Galveston, an act of God intervened in behalf of the businessmen. A short time before the charter election, Dayton suffered a devastating flood; when the mayor proved unable to cope with the problems it created, John H. Patterson took charge of the city. Patterson used his factory, fortunately located on high ground, as a rescue headquarters; quickly manufactured many makeshift boats; housed and fed flood victims; and as the waters receded stood out as hero and leader. In the election, the manager charter carried easily. . . .

[Commission and manager government had become the favorite of local business—because the new municipal governments met their most obvious needs. From the beginning the new form of government permitted substantial increases in the services provided by the city, at little or no extra cost, and often at considerable savings.]

\*          \*          \*

The argument that commission and manager charters would assure the election of "good" (i.e., business) men to office usually proved valid. The first commission in Galveston comprised five businessmen—"a veteran wholesale merchant," a "promising young . . . banker," "an active partner in a prosperous wholesale house," "a successful real estate dealer," and the secretary-treasurer of a livestock concern—all "good, clean, representative men." In Austin, Mayor A. P. Wooldrige, himself a prominent banker, headed a "businessman's government" that stayed in office for ten years. In Janesville, businessmen were in the leadership under both the commission and manager charters. In Dayton, John H. Patterson and the chamber of commerce put up a hand-picked slate that won easily. In Springfield, Ohio, five experienced businessmen made up the commission, while in Jackson, Michigan, most of the councilmen from 1914 to 1919 were business executives, bankers or merchants, and the mayor during these years was also president of the chamber of commerce. In Illinois, too, the new commissions generally included several active businessmen, some of whom had not previously been active in politics.

Even in cities where businessmen did not constitute a majority of its members, the commission remained strongly under their influence. In Des Moines, for example, the city council frequently met with the advisory board of the Commercial Club to consult on matters of public importance. In Omaha, the Commercial Club organized an advisory committee with the intention of meeting regularly with the seven-man commission, so that the commissioners might "profit by the advice of men who know." The logical culmination of this development occurred in Beaufort, South Carolina, where the offices of city manager and secretary of the board of trade were combined, with the city government and the local businessmen each paying one half the manager's salary. Commission and manager governments did, indeed, encourage businessmen to play a more direct role in municipal affairs.

This being so, most businessmen were well satisfied with the operation of the new form of municipal government. In 1915, in an effort to decide whether or not to sponsor a commission-manager charter in its city, the chamber of commerce of Fulton, New York, sent a confidential inquiry to bankers and other leading businessmen in cities that had adopted the manager plan. Replies were received from thirty-two cities. In twenty-eight, business leaders found the manager system highly satisfactory; in three they were disappointed; in one city they were divided.

Many reported substantial savings in the operation of their city government, while almost all boasted of increased services with no extra cost. Bank presidents and cashiers were almost unanimous in their praise of manager government. The assistant cashier of the River National Bank in Springfield, Ohio, wrote that "the business class of our citizens are very well satisfied." A bank president from Sherman, Texas, reported that "those who pay taxes are generally satisfied with the new system." The cashier of the Union Bank in Jackson, Michigan, wrote, "Its effect on business is favorable." From Montrose, Colorado, Charles A. Black replied, "I am one of the largest property owners and taxpayers here.

. . . I find that our present city manager government is far superior and more satisfactory all around." Finally, the city manager of Manistee, Michigan, advised: "You cannot make any mistake in adopting this business form of government."

[Reformers in organizations of the genteel, such as the National Municipal League, often praised commission and manager government in traditional terms—for its simplicity, its concentration of responsibility, its intelligibility to the average voter. But the main burden of defense of the new reform fell on business organizations, and they carried on the debate in business parlance.]

*    *    *

At the 1913 meeting of the League of Kansas Municipalities, the visiting secretary of the Iowa League argued that "a city is more than a business corporation," and that, while business principles should control financial actions, this was not the primary function of municipal government. "Good health," he concluded, "is more important than a low tax rate." The same year the Washington League of Municipalities convention heard Spokane's commissioner of public safety complain of the tendency to run municipal government from a "cold-blooded business standpoint." Municipal government, the commissioner observed, "is more than a mere organization for business."

[Other opponents, particularly political machines in Northern cities, Socialists, and trade unionists, had more specific grievances. Their fears and opposition came from a belief that the commission and manager charters would, by design or not, eliminate workers or their representatives from active participation in the process of government.]

The Socialist Party, which between 1910 and 1919 elected various municipal officers in over 300 cities, led in opposing many features of commission and manager plans. Three major features of the plans bore the brunt of Socialist criticism: the elimination of ward representation, which meant the end of minority representation; the extreme concentration of power in the hands of the commission, which meant quick decisions and little time to mobilize opposition; and the "fallacy" of the nonpartisan ballot, which meant the elimination of three-way contests for office and an emphasis on personality, rather than party.

One report of a Connecticut Socialist found that commission government was the product of the " 'merchant and capitalist class,' " and that commission-governed cities afforded a fine medium for " 'capitalists to advertise their business.' " In Pocatello, Idaho, the Socialist party took the lead in defeating a commission government charter, arguing that it was an " 'autocratic and exclusive form of city government.' " In Manitowoc, Wisconsin, where a Socialist was mayor, the party opposed a proposal for commission government and defeated the new charter by a vote of 298 to 1,049. In Hamilton, Ohio, a few days after the United States entered the First World War, the Socialists defeated an attempt to form a manager government. In Dayton, the Socialists became the main source of opposition to the manager charter, although the United Trades and Labor Council also opposed the new reform. There, the Socialists, Democrats, and Prohibitionists issued a pamphlet entitled *Dayton's Commission Manager Plan: Why Big Manufacturers, Bond Holders, and Public Franchise Grabbers Favor It, and Workingmen and Common People Oppose.*

The elimination of patronage undoubtedly moved political machines in many cities to oppose commission government, but the opposition of the Socialists and labor, neither of which had much patronage to lose, cannot be so easily dismissed. Several features of the electoral process in commission and manager cities did favor business groups against labor and its political allies. The first of these was simple limitation of the right to vote. In Galveston, the original plan provided for the appointment of all five commissioners. The state legislature modified this to provide for the election of two of the five, but it took a court decision decreeing appointive government unconstitutional to make the Galveston commission fully elective. In Houston, the second commission city, a poll tax of $2.50 limited democracy by eliminating 7,500 "irresponsible" voters in a potential electorate of 12,000. And in Newport, Rhode Island, there was a similar restriction of the right to vote. Overt limitation of suffrage, however, was out of keeping with the prevailing spirit of these years. Thus, when James G. Berryhill—himself a Progressive—introduced the plan in Des Moines, he added the initiative, the referendum, and the recall, as well as the nonpartisan ballot. These features became characteristic of commission and manager charters.

Nevertheless, the heart of the plan, that of electing only a few men on a citywide vote, made election of minority or labor candidates more difficult and less likely. Before the widespread adoption of commission and manager government it was common for workingmen to enter politics and serve as aldermen, or even mayor. Socialists elected teamsters, machinists, cigar makers, railroad conductors and trainmen, tinners, carpenters, miners, and other workers to the mayoralty of dozens of cities and towns in these years. But once the commission plan was in effect this became rare. Workingclass aldermen were hard hit because the resources needed to conduct a citywide campaign were much greater than those needed for a ward election, and because minorities—political, racial, or national—were usually concentrated in specific wards. In Dayton, for example, the Socialists received twenty-five percent of the vote in the election immediately preceding the adoption of the manager reform, electing two ward councilmen and three assessors. In 1913, after the manager charter was adopted, they received thirty-five percent of the vote and elected no one to the commission. In 1917 the party again increased its vote, this time to forty-four percent; again they elected no candidate.

The nonpartisan ballot, a feature of most commission-manager plans and widely heralded as a great advance in democracy, also tended to operate against minority groups. Socialists claimed that the nonpartisan ballot gave great advantage to men of wealth and prominence, and that it gave a "terrific advantage" to the commercial press—although in fact, the Socialist Party often maintained its strength better in nonpartisan elections than did the major parties which depended heavily on patronage to hold together their organizations. To some degree, however, the nonpartisan ballot did handicap the workingclass candidates—most of whom were known only in their own neighborhoods and were without access to the press or adequate campaign funds. Theirs was a double task: to present themselves and their principles to the public. The nonpartisan ballot was a boon to the well-known man, and the well-known man, more often than not, was a leading merchant, manufacturer, or the lawyer of one or the other. In addition, the combination of administrative and executive functions in the commission plan meant that the city could function smoothly only when experienced business executives were chosen to run it. The people of Wichita, Kansas, learned this when a former street laborer was elected to the commission. Being a street laborer, wrote reformer H. S. Gilbertson, was "an honest calling," and workers did have a right to representation. But, he asked, does this give "a man quite the preparation for managing one of the departments of a city?"

[Although the manager plan eliminated the problem of electing incompetent administrators, it strengthened the already strong tendency to regard the city as a "stock company." The method of electing the commission or council remained the same, and the manager, chosen by the commission or council, proved most often to be a man of limited social outlook, one who tended to think purely in business or, more narrowly, engineering terms. The reduction of expenditures made by the manager, while of great benefit to the taxpaying citizens, was often made at labor's expense. In Staunton, Virginia, for example, the new manager saved money by paying formerly full-time city employees only for those hours actually worked.]

The managers were usually proficient at increasing the efficiency of a fire department or reducing the cost of street paving, but social and political problems were often outside their range of interest. In 1918 Richard S. Childs (under whose direction H. S. Gilbertson had drawn up the Lockport Manager charter) suggested to the City Managers' Association, "Some day we shall have managers here who have achieved national reputation, not by . . . running their cities for a freakishly low expense per capita, but managers who have successfully led their commissions into great new enterprises of service." The advice was met with hostility. The managers, Leonard D. White notes, told Childs "directly that theorists were not welcome at the meetings of the Association." Civil engineering, not social engineering, interested the manager; economy, not service, was his basic principle.

Because of his training, the manager tended to share the corporate concept of the city: All elements of the community must be harmonized, but in the interest of the major stockholders. He identified with the growing tendency among Progressives to remove as many areas of social and economic decision making as possible from the realm of politics. An extreme statement of this view appeared in the magazine *Engineering and Contracting:* ". . . our entire system of 'representative government,' in which representation comes solely through elections, is an uneconomic system, and is destined shortly to be changed."

There were many, besides the Socialists, who thought commission government had already changed the system of representation and had guaranteed business rule. Most of these men did not oppose the new plans *in toto,* but only wished to assure that the commissions reflect the makeup of the entire community. To this end, they proposed proportional representation in the elections to the commission, and revived the Proportional Representation League to lead the fight.

The League, which had been in existence since the early 1890's, had lain dormant for many years. In 1914, a year after Dayton installed its first city manager, the *Proportional Representation Review* renewed publication, and that year and the next many new members joined the League's council. Active in the rejuvenated League were Progressives like John R. Commons, William S. U'Ren, Charles A. Beard, and Ben B. Lindsey. The genteel reformers were represented by Charles W. Eliot, Albert Shaw, Charles Francis Adams, and DeLancy Verplanck, and the Socialists by Carl D. Thompson and Charles P. Steinmetz. Despite the activity of the League, however, proportional representation made little headway. In the eight years from 1914 to 1922 only five cities adopted this reform.

In Dayton, where opposition to the unrepresentative council developed rapidly after the adoption of the manager charter, proportional representation failed because business groups opposed a reform which they believed could benefit only Socialists and Negroes.

Nor was the fear of the Dayton businessmen without basis. In Kalamazoo, in the first proportional representation election in 1918, Truxton Talbot, a "radical Socialist," was elected to the commission. Thereafter, the inclination of Kalamazoo's "really representative" commission to do something "more directly of benefit to the people than cleaning the streets and lighting them" disturbed the business interests of the city, or so the manager claimed. What happened in Kalamazoo must have confirmed the fears of many chambers of commerce and thereby strengthened their opposition to modifications of commission or manager charters. At any rate, the proportional representation movement had no more success than did Socialist and trade union attacks on the commission plans.

[Business leaders did not intend to share with other classes in their cities any more than was necessary. They were willing to make concessions on programs, however, particularly since many of the programs supported or demanded by reformers and workingmen made for greater efficiency and lessened class antagonisms. This led them, perhaps unknowingly in some instances, in the direction of municipal ownership, of increased planning, and, especially where the competition from radicals was keen, even toward social reform.] In Dayton, for example, after five years of manager government, municipal garbage collection had been instituted, a municipal asphalt plant built, new sewers (based on the projected needs of 1950) constructed, parks improved, new bridges erected, and a Department of Public Welfare established. The Welfare Department instituted milk inspection, free legal aid, a municipal employment agency, a municipal lodging house, medical examinations for school children, free vaccination, playgrounds, play festivals, and other social services, all on the theory that "happy workers are more efficient."

*         *         *

All commissions aimed to reduce costs and increase services, and, since these were their first principles, most followed a policy of municipal planning and municipal ownership of some, if not all, utilities. To a large degree, therefore, the programs of the various business groups which led the commission and manager movements had points in common with those of many social reformers, and even with those of the Socialists.

Fundamental differences between business groups and the genteel reformers, on the one hand, and Socialists, labor, and some of the more radical social reformers, on the other, did exist both in regard to what class should administer these programs, and what the ultimate purpose of the programs should be. But the similarity of many immediate goals often debilitated the political opposition and helped assure the adoption of the commission and manager charters. Developed and led by business groups, the movement fulfilled the requirements of progressivism by rationalizing city government and institutionalizing the methods and values of the corporations that had come to dominate American economic life. The end result of the movements was to place city government firmly in the hands of the business class. And, interestingly, at what is normally considered the end of the Progressive Era, 1917, the manager movement spurted ahead at its highest rate of growth. This occurred in the five years from 1918 to 1923, when 153 cities adopted manager charters, as compared to 87 in the five years before 1918, and 84 in the five years after 1923.

During the First World War, chambers of commerce and boards of trade greatly intensified their antiradical and antilabor activities, and in hundreds of small cities and towns Socialist locals were destroyed by the superpatriotic business groups. Just as the war would serve to institutionalize corporation-controlled regulatory agencies on a national level . . . so on a local level the business organizations were able rapidly to press forward their political domination of American municipalities.

*Louis Heaton Pink*

# SOCIALISM IN SCHENECTADY

*Louis Heaton Pink, an observer of Socialism in Schenectady, New York, during the Progressive era, describes municipal Socialism as similar to non-Socialist urban reform government. Commenting on the administration of Mayor George R. Lunn, Pink suggests that the tone of the administration might have differed from that of its predecessors but that social revolution was no closer in Schenectady than anywhere else in the nation.*

From Louis Heaton Pink, "Socialism on Trial," *The Outlook,* CV (November 1, 1913), pp. 489–492.

From New York to San Francisco, gesticulating street orators urge Schenectady as proof of successful Socialism. What has really been done in that little industrial city on the banks of the Mohawk? How does Socialist administration differ from any other?

When I came upon Walter Kruesi, Commissioner of Charities, he was sweeping out the municipal store in the basement of City Hall Annex. "We are a little short-handed to-day," he remarked, and went on with the job. The floor swept, we started upstairs. On the way we met an Italian woman with a mesh bag. "I came for some groceries," she said. "You are half an hour late, and the store is locked," said the Commissioner; "however, come on." He turned back, opened the store, and filled the mesh bag, which seemed capable of indefinite expansion. He was not cross or hurried, but suggested olive oil and macaroni when his customer had exhausted her wants.

Many of the callers in the Mayor's office were workmen in overalls. As I was talking with Mayor George R. Lunn, the janitor, brush in hand, came in to discuss the policy of the administration.

The workman feels that the government is his as much as the shop-owner's, and that he is an important part of the body politic. City officials look upon their work as a mission. Democracy is real, not simulated.

Otherwise this Socialist administration and a Democratic or Republican administration are the same. Social revolution and common ownership of the tools of production are no nearer in Schenectady than in New York or Chicago or Key West.

## The Big Things

The Socialist administration began January 1, 1912. I asked the Mayor what he considered the big things done. He answered:

(1) Solving the water problem.

(2) Increasing the pay of laborers.

(3) Establishing a garbage-disposal plant, and beginning the free collection of garbage, and ashes.

Schenectady owns its water system, but in 1903 made a contract with the Schenectady Railway Company—now the Schenectady Illuminating Company—to pump for the city system. For several years the company and the city have been at odds, each claiming breach of contract. The city has failed to provide adequate storage, and the company has not established proper pumping facilities and maintained adequate pressure. The city was growing fast, and the situation became dangerous. On July 28, 1913, the Common Council ratified an agreement with the company, which promised to erect new pumps and release the city from all claims for damages, the city binding itself to build a twelve-million-gallon storage reservoir.

When the Socialists found themselves at the helm, laborers were paid $1.75 a day. One of the first acts of the new administration was to raise the pay to $2. Last spring another increase was made to $2.25. The city compels contractors on municipal work to pay the same wage, so that the average rate in all employments has been affected. Mayor Lunn says that labor is better paid in Schenectady than in any other city in the State.

Schenectady has never before made provision for disposal of garbage. The State Board of Health long ago ordered the city to build a disposal plant, but only now is the work under way. A portion of an island in the Mohawk River has been purchased for the site and a contract for the plant has been let. Within another month the city will have taken over the collection of garbage and ashes. The superintendent, a practical wagon-builder, is constructing ash and garbage wagons by direct employment at a considerable saving to the city.

These are, in the eyes of the Mayor, the three "big things." There is nothing Socialistic about them. Any moderately progressive city would have done likewise. The remarkable thing is that these needs were not attended to years ago and that it was left to a chance Socialist administration to gain the credit for doing the obvious.

\*　　　\*　　　\*

## Steps Towards Socialism

Strange that in strict business matters the Socialists have made exceptional progress and in matters Socialistic they have failed, or nearly. In several instances all that saved them was an injunction from the hostile camp.

The municipal store and the sale of ice and coal by the city are steps towards Socialism. The city store sold about twenty per cent under the market rate. It had no rent to pay. It did not deliver. Hence its trade was small, about $300 a week. Then came the injunction. People who had never shown the slightest interest in the venture bemoaned the fact that the privilege of buying at cost was denied them. Nothing became it like its death. The store is now an adjunct of the Charities Department; through it provisions are given to the poor instead of money.

On June 1, 1912, the city began peddling ice. The price was reduced about forty per cent, and a large clientele among the poorer people was soon built up. On the 4th of July came an injunction—fortunately, for the city was losing money. The work was badly organized. It is no easy job for the city to compete with the iceman; to succeed it must have a monopoly. If the city had a monopoly of the ice and coal business, say the Socialists, it could cut the cost almost in half.

Coal is still sold. To avoid an injunction the business was taken out of the hands of the city and put in charge of an organization of Socialist office-holders called the Lunn Associates. From fifty to seventy-five cents a ton is saved to the purchaser. The Lunn Associates have had their troubles with inferior coal and slack business methods, but now they are well organized and moderately successful.

## The Mayor

The sparking-plug of the Socialist machine, the Mayor, is tall, thin, distinguished-looking; clean shaven, boyish, well dressed. He has an engaging smile. He runs rapidly over the scale from comic to serious and back again. He rams home his arguments with gestures, has a splendid voice and an eye that holds. Impetuous, full of fun, bubbling over with boyish enthusiasm, rushing pell-mell into some serious difficulty and smiling and bluffing his way out, courageous to a fault, by many considered the best orator in New York State, Mayor Lunn is a power to be reckoned with.

Few dime-novel heroes have had careers more varied than his.

He was called to Schenectady to become the pastor of the First Reformed Church, a wealthy parish, the front pews filled by the best families, many of them descendants from the old Dutch settlers. Lunn spoke from the shoulder. He preached Christian Socialism.

Soon the church was in uproar. There was the Lunn or radical faction and the conservative element. Forced out, Lunn consolidated
two dwindling congregations into the United People's Church. Here
too a rift soon appeared. To this day the anti-Lunn faction uses the
church at night and the Mayor preaches in the forenoon.

Lunn not only split open his churches, but the whole town took
sides. To aid his fight Dr. Lunn purchased the "Citizen," a weekly
paper, and made it the Socialist organ. This brought him a wider
audience. He was nominated for Mayor in the fall of 1911; the
people were disgusted with both old parties, the star of destiny
twinkled, and, much to the surprise of every one, including the
pastor-editor, he was elected.

"What are the big obstacles you have encountered?" I asked the
Mayor.

"Whenever we try to do anything," he answered, "we run up
against the Charter. It is an oak charter, fixed and immovable. It is,
by all means, the one great obstacle we have had to overcome. Our
second greatest trouble has been pettifogging politicians, the 'old
guard.' They have done everything possible to block us. Take the
matter of injunctions. My drawer is full of them. The wonder is that
we have been able to do anything, hampered this way."

That very instant the "old guard" was seeking the arrest of the
Mayor because he had with his own hands chopped down an in-
junction-protected tree in the center of the sidewalk which impeded
the work of laying water mains.

"Do you know," said the Mayor, with quiet earnestness, "they
charge me with being against law? I am not. I believe in law. The
more I see law abused, the more I believe in it. Law should be for
the protection of the people, it should not be abused. It should be
another name for justice. Law is the shell, justice is the kernel. It
is the kernel that is alive, the shell is a mere covering. Sometimes it
may be necessary to break the shell to give the kernel room to grow.
Law should accommodate itself to justice."

From law he turned to Christianity.

"Christianity is service," mused the Mayor. "Often those who do
not profess Christianity, because they do not understand its forms,
are the best Christians. They are the servants of their fellows. Law
and Christianity are the foundations of the Socialist State. We can't

inaugurate Socialism here. No city or group of cities can do it. But we can show the people that Socialism is not dangerous. Why, many prophesied ruin for the city when we came into power. Instead, Schenectady has grown as never before."

*David A. Shannon*

# VICTOR L. BERGER, SOCIALIST BOSS OF MILWAUKEE

*In his study of* The Socialist Party of America, *historian David A. Shannon describes municipal Socialism in Milwaukee, where for many years it was a strong political force. Allied with the local trade unions and based on the city's German-Americans, the Milwaukee Socialists, under the leadership of Victor L. Berger, built an efficient political machine. According to Shannon, Socialist Berger was "one of the bossiest 'bosses' in a nation that has developed the art to a high degree." Professor Shannon has authored* The Socialist Party of America *and* The Decline of American Communism *as well as other works about the United States in the twentieth century.*

The history of Milwaukee Socialism is largely the story of Victor L. Berger, one of the giants of the American movement. Scholarly in appearence as only a Teutonic secondary schoolteacher can be, dignified to the point that his enemies considered him pompous, and with so little humor that the heavy-handed attempts at lightheartedness in his writing were pathetic, this Austrian immigrant was the most able machine politician and organizer in the party. His contributions to the party were not in his journalism, although he published German and English Socialist newspapers in Milwaukee throughout his career, nor in his role as a congressman, but in his welding together a strong political machine that to this day is a force in Milwaukee. More radical members of the party were disgusted with Milwaukee's caution, with its gradual "step at a time" policies, and with its general stuffiness—Trotsky's jibe that a convention of

American Socialists looked like a meeting of dentists, while not a valid comment for the wild Westerners, certainly was an apt description of Milwaukee delegations—but the Milwaukee Socialists did build an organization that was successful politically.

The secret of the success of the Milwaukee Socialists was their close alliance with the trade unions. Milwaukee AFL men were Socialists. Berger's newspaper, the *Social Democratic Herald,* carried on its masthead the legend "Official paper of the Federated Trades Council of Milwaukee and of the Wisconsin State Federation of Labor." Popularity of the Socialist Party in the Milwaukee labor movement did not come of any "boring from within," of parliamentary trickery whereby the unions were put on record as supporters of Socialism, but by Socialists working hard in the trade union movement, getting the confidence and respect of the unionists, and converting them to their way of thought. Berger many times heatedly denounced efforts to "bore from within" in the sense of winning a vote or passing a pro-Socialist resolution. In writing of Max Hayes's unsuccessful attempt to get a pro-Socialist resolution through the 1902 AFL convention, Berger declared: "A resolution like this, even when [if] passed with a large majority, would mean little or nothing to the cause of Socialism in America. In fact experience in the past . . . has proven that resolutions of trades union congresses, even when going so far as to advise the members to vote the ticket of the Socialist party, amount to nothing in practice." Labor support of Socialism had to be freely given and genuine to have any value; anything else would be only a paper victory.

Labor support alone, however, was not enough to win elections. A strong party organization of the kind major parties use so successfully was another necessity. The Milwaukee Socialists had a party organization in every precinct to get their supporters registered, get them to the polls, and get their ballots counted. The party machinery could get literature into every house in Milwaukee within a few hours and in the proper language, English, German, or Polish. Victor Berger was the "boss" behind all these party activities and one of the bossiest "bosses" in a nation that had developed the art to a high degree. The Berger machine offered the Milwaukee electorate entertainment just as other political organizations realize the political possibilities of Roman circuses. In 1902, for example, Milwaukee

Socialists offered the public a baseball game between the north-side and south-side Socialist organizations. The tickets were embellished with the red flag, and the *Herald* undoubtedly stimulated attendance when it announced that none other than Berger himself would be on the field as a substitute for the north siders. The box score of the game discloses that Berger did not get into the game even as a pinch hitter, but the sight of the Socialist "boss" in a baseball uniform, lager physique and all, must have been well worth the price of admission.

Another factor in the Milwaukee Socialists' success was their appeal to that city's peculiar ethnic composition. There were and are three main ethnic groups in Milwaukee: the Yankees, the Germans, and the Poles. The Socialists had tremendous strength among the Germans, substantial influence among the Yankees, and their least power among the Poles. The Socialist membership was overwhelmingly German, so much so that there were many jokes among the Socialists in other parts of the country about their Teutonic Wisconsin comrades. One of these had to do with the Milwaukee Socialist who was explaining the failure of a Socialist candidate with a Polish name to win an election. "If we had had someone with a good American name like Schemmelpfennig we could have won." Yet there were representatives of old Yankee stock prominent in the Milwaukee movement. Frederic Heath, whose forefathers on both sides of his family has crossed the Atlantic on the *Mayflower,* was editor of the *Herald,* and Carl D. Thompson, a former Congregational minister, held public office under Socialist auspices. The party's strongest Polish leader was Leo Krzycki of the Amalgamated Clothing Workers.

With its emphasis upon winning elections and its alliance with the local AFL unions, it is not surprising that Milwaukee Socialists were cautious evolutionary social democrats. If the Milwaukee Socialist leadership was to maintain its political strength and its trade union support, it could not get very far ahead of dominant social attitudes in the city. The Milwaukee organization was vigorously opposed to the IWW from its very beginning, and critical of those Socialists, including Debs, who supported the Wobblies. The *Herald* referred to the IWW's first convention as the "anti-A.F. of L. convention," and criticized what it considered the well meaning but misguided Socialists in attendance "who have allowed their feelings against Gomperism to be played upon to draw them out of the inside fight of [with] the A.F. of L.'s capitalistic misleaders—deserting the fight where it should be waged in order to impotently make faces at Gompers from the outside." This was the kernel of Milwaukee Socialism's labor principles: opposition to Gompers but dedication to the idea of winning the AFL to Socialism from the inside rather than fighting it from the outside.

*Roy Lubove*

# THE PITTSBURGH RENAISSANCE—AN EXAMPLE OF THE REVERSE WELFARE STATE

*This selection from Roy Lubove's study of* Twentieth Century Pittsburgh *demonstrates that business-inspired urban reform was not limited to the Progressive era. Studying the Pittsburgh Renaissance of the post-World War II period, Lubove finds that the city's corporate elite, once reluctant to use public resources and thereby expand government intervention, changed its point of view. In this way, corporate needs were served by public investment, and a reverse welfare state was established. In the light of recent developments in America's cities, the student might consider the impact of business-oriented renewal upon urban society; for example, is the ghetto dweller aided by new office buildings? Professor Lubove specializes in American urban and social history. His works include* The Progressives and the Slums *and* Twentieth Century Pittsburgh: Government, Business and Environmental Change.

In explaining the origins of Pittsburgh's massive physical renewal program following World War II, one cannot exaggerate the importance of the crisis atmosphere that pervaded the community. This led to drastic modification of the historic formula that had delegated constructive responsibility for intervention to voluntary institutions. The foundation of the entire Renaissance effort was the use of public powers and resources to preserve the economic vitality of the central business district (CBD) and, more broadly, the competitive economic position of the Pittsburgh region. In essence, the Pittsburgh Renaissance represented a response to a crisis situation, one that precipitated a dramatic expansion of public enterprise and investment to serve corporate needs; it established a reverse welfare state.

There is no doubt that Pittsburgh confronted disaster in the 1940's. Despite record wartime production and employment, the district could "boast of few important new industries, and the gain in population has been limited." Many persons "have been apprehensive—some of them definitely pessimistic—regarding the prospects for the Pittsburgh district." By 1945 "large corporations which had long made their headquarters in Pittsburgh had actually taken options on properties in other cities and were laying plans to build skyscrapers there and move their offices." These included Westinghouse, Alcoa, and U.S. Steel. Corporate managerial and technical personnel and their wives "didn't want to live and raise their families under . . . prevailing environmental conditions." A blanket of smoke choked "the city much of the time. There are floods almost every year. Hundreds of communities dump their raw sewage into Pittsburgh's rivers. . . . Housing is substandard. No major highway has been built and none is in design." Pittsburgh, in short, was "not a fit place in which to live and work and raise a family. That being the case, the responsible citizenry of the city faced a tough decision. No longer could they vacillate, rationalize, compromise. . . . Either they would stay and eventually rebuild the core of the central city, or they would get out and take their industries with them."

One crucial circumstance that influenced the future of Pittsburgh was the assumption by a "whole group of young leaders" of "positions of executive responsibility and power." Their emergence and involvement in the creation of Pittsburgh's reverse welfare state was, in turn, associated with one man's decision to rebuild rather than abandon Pittsburgh. Richard King Mellon assumed control of the family enterprises in the late 1930's, following the death of his father, Richard Beaty, and uncle, Andrew. In 1946 the family interests were consolidated in T. Mellon and Sons, and new executives arrived in Pittsburgh to head the Mellon concerns: General Brehon Somervell at Koppers; George H. Love at Pittsburgh Consolidation Coal; Frank Denton at Mellon Bank; and Sidney W. Swensrud at Gulf Oil. "The blunt fact about Pittsburgh's changing scene," *Fortune* reported, "is that a new generation is in power. . . . It begins in the Mellon empire, extends through Big Steel, and runs through the other power groupings."

The main vehicle through which the new corporate elite participated in the Renaissance effort was the Allegheny Conference on Community Development (ACCD). It was established in 1943 when Mellon convened a small group to discuss Pittsburgh's future. From the conference evolved the idea of "forming a non-profit, non-partisan civic organization, to be devoted to research and planning, to develop an over all community improvement program." Wallace Richards, director of the Pittsburgh Regional Planning Association since 1937, played a key role in establishing the ACCD. Mellon had become president of the agency in 1941, and Richards emphasized to him the need for a comprehensive postwar planning program. Richards' involvement suggests that the ACCD was the product of professional as well as top corporate initiative. Dr. Robert E. Doherty, president of Carnegie Tech, and Dr. Edward Weidlein, director of Mellon Institute, were both prominent in the early planning and administration of the Conference; it became an effective force after Park H. Martin, an engineer-planner, was appointed executive director in 1945.

Civic organization in Pittsburgh was not new; Pittsburgh and other American cities were the graveyard of citizen organizations established to promote environmental or social change. What made the ACCD unique was its success, and this requires explanation. Richard Mellon's leadership and the recruitment of the corporate elite provided the ACCD with extraordinary potential power; but a policy decision adopted when the Conference was first established in 1943 insured that the power would be exercised. This was the requirement that members of the executive committee participate personally in its deliberations, and as individuals rather than representatives of any corporation.

The Conference's effectiveness was also associated with its use of technical and professional skills. The ACCD established close ties to the leading planning and research agencies of the areas, including the Pittsburgh Regional Planning Association and Pennsylvania Economy League, Western Division. Indeed, the Pittsburgh Regional served, for all practical purposes, as the technical and planning arm of the ACCD. The ACCD did not simply advocate general policies; it sponsored concrete, detailed plans prepared by engineers, architects, economists, and other experts. This ability to command unlimited technical skills contrasted sharply with most civic organizations, and especially with neighborhood citizens' groups.

The policy statements and plans of the ACCD were not only preceded by extensive research, but also by consultation with the voluntary and public agencies affected by any proposal. The same strategy of consensus was used with the local press. By avoiding public controversy, the ACCD could more readily identify its programs with the community interest.

The effectiveness of the ACCD depended ultimately upon the cooperation of Mayor David Lawrence and the City-County Democratic political machine. "The future," as Lawrence explained, "was to establish the working relationships between the Democratic administration and Richard Mellon." Lawrence paid particular tribute to Richards and to Mellon adviser Arthur B. Van Buskirk as the men who most "sensed the necessity of uniting public and private action for Pittsburgh's advancement." Through their efforts in large measure, Pittsburgh pioneered "in municipal techniques which have since become commonplace." These techniques included extensive use of the "authority" mechanism in the renewal process and dependence upon the resources of every level of government. Thus the Pittsburgh civic coalition linked Democrat and Republican, businessman and politician, federal, state, and local government; and it adopted any administrative expedient that would serve its purpose.

Finally, the ACCD was successful because it forged a consensus on community policy. The ACCD could mold a powerful civic coalition because no one seriously challenged its proposition that the goal of community policy was revitalization of the CBD and ultimately the regional economy. "The need for preserving and protecting the stability of the Golden Triangle," Park Martin emphasized, "was recognized and accepted, and the program deliberately placed great emphasis on this area." Public officials agreed with the "civic leaders" that "the values of the Downtown must be preserved and strengthened before all else."

The establishment of the reverse welfare state, and the prestige of the ACCD, hinged upon three projects in the early days of the Renaissance. All three—Point Park, smoke control, and flood control—had long been advocated in Pittsburgh, and they demonstrated the use of public power or investment to promote private economic ends. As Wallace Richards explained, "the enterprise system itself has sought and established in Pittsburgh a partnership between private business and all levels of government." The irony of the environmental change process in twentieth century Pittsburgh was not that it ultimately hinged upon constructive public intervention, but that use of public resources was so closely identified with the corporate welfare.

# Suggestions for Additional Reading

For views of machine politics by those living during the late nineteenth and early twentieth century, students should consult the following works: James Bryce, *The American Commonwealth* (New York, 1893); M. Ostrogorski, *Democracy and the Organization of Political Parties,* Volume II, *The United States,* edited and abridged by Seymour Martin Lipset (Chicago, 1964), especially Chapters Six and Seven of Part Five; Lincoln Steffens, *The Shame of the Cities* (New York, 1957) and *The Autobiography of Lincoln Steffens* (New York, 1931); and William L. Riordon, *Plunkitt of Tammany Hall* (New York, 1948). Of these, Ostrogorski, who first published in 1902, is the most objective and analytical. In 1919, Samuel P. Orth contributed Volume 43, *The Boss and the Machine: A Chronicle of Politicians and Party Organization* (New Haven, 1919) to *The Chronicles of America Series*. This book gives the scholarly view of bossism at the end of the Progressive era.

During the 1930's, several political scientists investigated urban machine politics. Biographical portraits of individual bosses can be found in Harold Zink, *City Bosses in the United States: A Study of Twenty Municipal Bosses* (Durham, North Carolina, 1930). Shortly after Zink's work appeared, J. T. Salter published *Boss Rule: Portraits in City Politics* (New York, 1935), and Harold F. Gosnell wrote *Machine Politics: Chicago Model* (Chicago, 1937). Subsequently, individual bosses were considered in Walton Bean, *Boss Ruef's San Francisco* (Berkeley, 1952) and a decade later in political scientist Alex Gottfried's *Boss Cermak of Chicago: A Study of Political Leadership* (Seattle, 1962). In more recent years, political scientists have investigated the broad question of machine politics in the May 1964 issue of *The Annals* entitled "City Bosses and Political Machines."

Since the middle of the 1960's, historians, reflecting an increased interest in American urban history, have given more and more attention to city politics. The famous William Marcy Tweed and his city are the subject of two works, Seymour Mandelbaum's *Boss Tweed's New York* (New York, 1965) and Alexander B. Callow, Jr.'s *The Tweed Ring* (New York, 1966). In *Tammany: The Evolution of a Political Machine, 1789–1865* (Syracuse, 1971), Jerome Mushkat considers the origins of the Hall. An early muckraking investigation can be found in M.R. Werner, *Tammany Hall* (New York, 1928); a portrait of Tweed himself is in Dennis Tilden Lynch's *"Boss" Tweed: The Story of a Grim Generation* (New York, 1927). Later New York politics is investigated in Nancy Joan Weiss, *Charles Francis Murphy, 1858–1924: Respectability and Responsibility in Tammany Politics* (Northampton, Mass., 1968). This book contends, as does J. Joseph Huthmacher in the selection included in this volume, that in the case of Boss Murphy the line between boss and reformer was indeed a narrow one. To bring Tammany politics further up to date, see the memoirs of two of New York City's practicing politicians: Edward J. Flynn, *You're the Boss: The Practice of American Politics* (New York, 1962) and Edward N. Costikyan, *Behind Closed Doors: Politics in the Public Interest* (New York, 1966).

Zane L. Miller, using the periphery-versus-center model of urban politics, sees the boss as a reformer in *Boss Cox's Cincinnati: Urban Politics in the Progressive Era* (New York, 1968); conversely, Melvin G. Holli contends that the reformer often had to use machine techniques in his *Reform in Detroit: Hazen S. Pingree and Urban Politics* (New York, 1969). The relationship of the boss and the settlement-house worker is examined in Allen F. Davis, *Spearheads for Reform: The Social Settlements and the Progressive Movement, 1890–1914* (New York, 1967). Machine politics in Kansas City and Chicago has received attention in recent works by Lyle Dorsett, *The Pendergast Machine* (New York, 1968), and Joel A. Tarr, *A Study in Boss Politics: William Lorimer of Chicago* (Urbana, Ill., 1971).

In his article "The Study of Corruption," *Political Science Quarterly* (December 1957), pp. 502–514, which is included in this anthology, Eric McKitrick raises the question of the changing nature of the political machine during the twentieth century. Many observers, in accord with the thesis of novelist Edwin O'Connor's *The Last Hurrah* (New York, 1956), believe that this change was one of weakening and decline for bossism in recent America. According to this view, the federal government, as a result of the New Deal, pre-empted the boss's social welfare service and thereby removed one of the significant latent functions described by Robert K. Merton in *Social Theory and Social Structure* (New York, 1957). Thus, the lessening need to go to the machine for welfare assistance, the alleged assimilation of ethnic groups, and the increase in civil service and the concomitant decline in patronage jobs all supposedly weakened machine politics in post-New Deal America. For a contrary interpretation applied to one city, see Bruce M. Stave, *The New Deal and the Last Hurrah: Pittsburgh Machine Politics* (Pittsburgh, 1970). This book contends that the New Deal relief and welfare programs assisted, rather than obstructed, the building of a Democratic political machine.

The effect of the welfare state on urban politics is also discussed in Harvey Wheeler, "Yesterday's Robin Hood: The Rise and Fall of Baltimore's Trenton Democratic Club," *American Quarterly*, VII (Winter 1955), pp. 332–344. In "The Politics of Urban Change", *Current History*, (December 1968), pp. 327–332, 365–366, Peter A. Lupsha considers the implications for contemporary America of bossism, the reform ethic, and the rise of the new communications media which has "turned our commitments outward from the local community to the national polity, and to the view that the city is more a political marketplace than a political community." Two recent popular accounts of a contemporary boss are William F. Gleason's *Daley of Chicago: The Man, the Mayor, and the Limits of Conventional Politics* (New York, 1970) and Mike Royko, *Boss: Richard J. Daley of Chicago* (New York, 1971). The mayor's views on politics and life have been compiled by Peter Yessne in *Quotations from Mayor Daley* (New York, 1969), which is perhaps a modern-day successor to *Plunkitt of Tammany Hall.*

Finally, urban structural reform during the Progressive era has been discussed in Harold A. Stone *et al., City Manager Government in the United States* (Chicago, 1940) and *City Manager Government in Nine Cities* (Chicago, 1940) and by Frederick C. Mosher *et al., City Manager Government in Seven Cities* (Chicago, 1940). To explore the relation of businessmen to Progressive reform, in addition to the articles by Hays and Weinstein reprinted herein, see Robert H. Wiebe, *Businessmen and Reform: A Study of the Progressive Movement* (Cambridge, 1962); Gabriel Kolko, *The Triumph of Conservatism: A Reinterpretation of American History, 1900–1916* (Chicago, 1967); and James Weinstein, *The Corporate Ideal in the Liberal State, 1900–1918* (Boston, 1969). The story of urban reform in one city is brought up to date by Roy Lubove's *Twentieth Century Pittsburgh: Government, Business and Environmental Change* (New York, 1969), in which he relates businessmen reformers to post-World War II America.

James Weinstein has also written about American Socialism in *The Decline of Socialism in America, 1912–1925* (New York, 1967). This work, as well as David A. Shannon's *The Socialist Party of America* (New York, 1955) and Daniel Bell's *Marxian Socialism in the United States* (Princeton, 1967), give passing reference to municipal Socialism; Henry F. Bedford, *Socialism and the Workers in Massachusetts, 1886–1912* (Amherst, Massachusetts, 1966), is a more specialized account. Several helpful articles which consider socialism in the cities are: Frederick I. Olson, "Milwaukee's First Socialist Administration, 1910–1912: A Political Evaluation," *Mid-America* (July 1961), pp. 197–207; Melvyn Dubofsky, "Success and Failure of Socialism in New York City, 1900–1918: A Case Study," *Labor History* (Fall 1968), pp. 361–375.

2   3   4   5   6   7   8   9   10